Beginning a career in teaching can be overwhelming—Melanie Meehan answers some of the most common questions writing teachers are tackling with a thoughtful approach for turning research into practice in every elementary classroom and empowering early career educators.

—Paula Bourque
Author of *Spark! Quick Writes to Kindle Hearts and Minds in Elementary Classrooms* and *Close Writing: Developing Purposeful Writers in Grades 2–6*

We learn best from each other, and Melanie Meehan does a phenomenal job of emphasizing how writers of all ages grow and learn from constructive criticism, feedback, and thoughtful responders. This is how we learn the importance of a growth mindset and learning how to make connections to our communities and the world around us. Teachers of all years and walks of life will walk away empowered and ready to grow their students across the curriculum.

—Darius Phelps
GAEYC 2016 Childcare Giver of the Year, Educator, Writer, Poet, and Illustrator

New teachers or new-to-workshop teachers will *hugely* benefit from this text. It gives a high-level overview of strong teaching practices—each supported with examples— and it gives a strong foundation for building a practice that's responsive to students' growth and learning while also being instructionally strong.

—Katie McGrath
Instructional Facilitator
Loudoun County Public Schools

Melanie Meehan masterfully weaves together relevant research, classroom examples, and her own experience as a writing mentor, coach, and teacher to paint a picture of the teaching of writing with students at the center. This is the book I wish I had as a new teacher and one I will turn to again and again in mentoring teachers who are new to writing or who want to develop a more meaningful writing instructional practice in their classrooms.

—Christina Nosek
Classroom Teacher and Author

In this not-to-be-missed guide to all-things-writing-workshop, Melanie Meehan thoughtfully shares ideas for creating a classroom community, what to teach writers, different methods of instruction, how to use assessment to move students forward, and ways to help students develop agency as writers and learners. *Answers to Your Biggest Questions About Teaching Elementary Writing* is a book teachers will turn to again and again for guidance, wisdom, tips, tools, and strategies for helping students develop as writers.

—Kathleen Neagle Sokolowski
Third-Grade Teacher

T0354080

Melanie Meehan emphasizes that building a supportive community of writers starts with teachers who write, as this creates a more responsive and reflective teacher who is ready to support a variety of writing needs. *Answers to Your Biggest Questions About Teaching Elementary Writing* will leave teachers feeling like they are writers. In turn, the students in front of them will share in honoring, reflecting, and cherishing their identity as writers, too.

—Allie Woodruff
First-Grade Classroom Teacher

Answers to Your Biggest Questions About Teaching Elementary Writing is not a book about finding what is wrong in student writing and correcting it; this is a book about using every avenue possible—whole group instruction, small group instruction, partner work, charts, thoughtful language (to name just a few!)—to discover all that students know and are able to do, and to invite them into co-crafting the instruction that matches their goals and their aspirations. Not satisfied with dreaming about the kind of writing instruction every child deserves, Melanie Meehan has written the book that maps out how to become a writing teacher worthy of the children we are privileged to teach.

—Shana Frazin
Co-Author, *Unlocking the Power of Classroom Talk*

ANSWERS *to Your* BIGGEST QUESTIONS *About*

TEACHING ELEMENTARY WRITING

This book is dedicated to every teacher who wonders, reflects, and commits to teaching children how to tell their stories and share their wisdom.

FIVE to THRIVE

ANSWERS *to Your*
BIGGEST QUESTIONS *About*

TEACHING ELEMENTARY WRITING

Melanie Meehan

CORWIN

For information:

Corwin
A SAGE Company
2455 Teller Road
Thousand Oaks, California 91320
(800) 233–9936
www.corwin.com

SAGE Publications Ltd.
1 Oliver's Yard
55 City Road
London EC1Y 1SP
United Kingdom

SAGE Publications India Pvt. Ltd.
B 1/I 1 Mohan Cooperative
Industrial Area
Mathura Road, New Delhi 110 044
India

SAGE Publications
Asia-Pacific Pte. Ltd.
18 Cross Street #10–10/11/12
China Square Central
Singapore 048423

President: Mike Soules
Vice President and Editorial Director:
    Monica Eckman
Executive Editor: Tori Mello Bachman
Content Development
    Editor: Sharon Wu
Editorial Assistant: Nancy Chung
Production Editor: Melanie Birdsall
Copy Editor: Deanna Noga
Typesetter: Integra
Proofreader: Lawrence W. Baker
Indexer: Maria Sosnowski
Cover Designer: Gail Buschman
Marketing Manager:
    Margaret O'Connor

Library of Congress Cataloging-in-Publication Data

Names: Meehan, Melanie, author.
Title: Answers to your biggest questions about teaching elementary writing : five to thrive / Melanie Meehan.
Description: Thousand Oaks, California : Corwin, 2022. | Series: Corwin literacy
Identifiers: LCCN 2021060911 (print) | LCCN 2021060912 (ebook) | ISBN 9781071858028 (paperback) | ISBN 9781071877012 (epub) | ISBN 9781071877036 (epub) | ISBN 9781071877043 (adobe pdf)
Subjects: LCSH: Language arts (Elementary) | English language--Composition and exercises--Study and teaching (Elementary)
Classification: LCC LB1576 .M4338 2022 (print) | LCC LB1576 (ebook) | DDC 372.6/044--dc23/eng/20220106
LC record available at https://lccn.loc.gov/2021060911
LC ebook record available at https://lccn.loc.gov/2021060912

This book is printed on acid-free paper.

22 23 24 25 26 10 9 8 7 6 5 4 3 2 1

CONTENTS

Visit the companion website at
resources.corwin.com/answerselementarywriting
for additional resources.

ACKNOWLEDGMENTS

First and foremost, a huge thank you and high five to Tori Bachman, editor extraordinaire, for trusting me with this project and keeping me on track to get it done! You make my work so much better, and I appreciate you. Additional gratitude to everyone at Corwin Press who has played a role in getting this book and series into the hands of teachers. Sharon Wu, Nancy Chung, Melanie Birdsall, and Deanna Noga, I admire and thank you for your attention to every detail. Margaret O'Connor and Sophie Zepf, thank you for your creative, enthusiastic promotional ideas.

Christina Nosek, you're an inspiring partner—thank you for the wine, coffee, nudges, and encouragement when I needed it most. I would not be brave enough to write books without the camaraderie of the co-authors of *Two Writing Teachers*. Much gratitude to Stacey Shubitz, Betsy Hubbard, Beth Moore, Kathleen Sokoloski, Therapi Kaplan, Amy Ellerman, Lainie Levin, and Nawal Qarooni Casiano—you are amazing collaborators! My colleagues in Simsbury continually push my thinking, especially my team of language arts consultants. Christine Neskie, Melanie Swider, Sharyl Panyard, Sarah McHugh, Diana Smith, Kathryn Anastasio, and our leader, Betsy Gunsalus—I have deep admiration and appreciation of your wisdom of all things literary and your commitment to student learning. This book would not exist without the students who teach me and the teachers who welcome me into their learning spaces. I'm sending a special thank you to Missie Champagne, my colleague across the hall, who always makes time to process, reflect, and deepen my thinking.

Books take a lot of time, and my husband and daughters share me with the computer when I'm in the midst of writing one. Thank you, Garth, Larkin, Julia, Clare, and Cecily—you are the best family ever!

PUBLISHER'S ACKNOWLEDGMENTS

Corwin gratefully acknowledges the contributions of the following reviewers:

Paula Bourque
Literacy Coach/Stenhouse Author
Augusta, Maine

Darius Phelps
Middle Grade Teacher and PhD Student
New York, New York

ABOUT THE AUTHOR

 **Melanie Meehan** has been the elementary writing and social studies coordinator in Simsbury, Connecticut, since 2012. Within that position, she writes curriculum, works with teachers, and strives to send students off into the world as confident writers who love to express their ideas. Melanie is a co-author of *Two Writing Teachers*, a blog dedicated to the teaching of writing, as well as a regular contributor to *Choice Literacy*. She wrote *Every Child Can Write,* which was published by Corwin Press in October 2019, and she co-authored *The Responsive Writing Teacher* with Kelsey Sorum, which was published in 2021. You can reach Melanie on Twitter, @MelanieMeehan1.

My teaching career began at an on-grounds school for children who had been removed from their homes for a variety of reasons. Many of the children harbored anger and grief due to the trauma they'd experienced. My co-teacher, Anne, and I knew writing could become an outlet, but we weren't sure how to structure meaningful writing instruction as the authentic communication form it could be. In search of ideas and inspiration, we attended a weeklong workshop that introduced us to many of the principles that have stayed with me throughout my teaching career. Writers have many specific, personal needs—cookies, coffee, a particular chair. However, the following core beliefs about writers' *fundamental* needs have not changed much, and they have anchored my thinking, approach, and action whenever I am working with or for students.

CORE BELIEFS ABOUT WRITERS' NEEDS

BELIEF 1: WRITERS NEED CHOICE

Our leaders emphasized the importance of choice, beginning even with the notebooks and pens we used. I spent time in a local store selecting a notebook that I still have today. It has no lines, thick paper, and a spiral binding so it can lie flat on either side. This notebook remains my favorite of all my notebooks, and I still bring it into classrooms for demonstration lessons. My favorite pens were felt, but with a fine tip and the ability to write smoothly, and I loved having different colors. Whenever I work with students, regardless of age and writing experiences, I provide options for pens, and I'm always amazed at how a new pen can jump-start a writer!

Choices exist in many aspects of writing, but perhaps the most important encompasses topic. During the workshop, our presenters continued to provide choice about how we thought of topics and what we wrote. Topic choice was critical for us, and it is critical for students who are discovering meaningful moments and topics for themselves. With time to explore, we came up with what mattered to us without knowing at the onset. We needed that time, though, because it allowed us to explore different topics and find patterns or themes for ourselves. We made lists, wrote off favorite quotes, and found passages we liked and tried to emulate them. These processes led to discovery and authentic topics. Just as the adults in my workshop wrote to discover, students also benefit from these processes.

BELIEF 2: WRITERS NEED TEACHERS WHO WRITE

During that weeklong writing workshop, the presenters intentionally provided time for participants to write. "You need to experience how it feels to do the work," they said. Since then, I have heard many other presenters say similar things: *Spy on yourself. Think about the thought processes you are engaging and the cognitive work you are doing, since that's what students will be experiencing as well.*

In a report published for the Department of Education, Graham (2012) provides several recommendations about writing instruction for students, asserting that students need to feel a sense of community as writers. The teacher is the lead learner, and if you're not writing, then you're missing out on a key element of building that community.

In addition to creating the community, teachers who write understand the synergy and pitfalls of writing. During my weeklong workshop, *we wrote*. My own personal life as a writer has become the most important element of my writing instruction. Donald Graves (n.d.b), a master teacher of writing and an important contributor in the field of research about writing instruction, said, "You can't ask someone to sing a duet with you until you know the tune yourself."

"I'm not a writer" is a phrase I hear often from teachers, and I understand why anyone would say it. I've written countless blog posts, a few novels (still unpublished), and a couple of professional books, and I still have moments when I feel like I can't write and I'm not a writer. Furthermore, writing is different from reading because if there's a book that's not engaging me, I can pick up a different one. There are times as a writer when I just can't get going.

But eventually, I do.

And it's in those places and spaces of feeling like I'm not a writer that I learn the most about how to teach writing.

BELIEF 3: WRITERS NEED TIME TO WRITE

Many writers will tell you that the secret to writing is ... writing. Stephen King is quoted as saying that if you want to be a good writer, you must do two things: read a lot and write a lot. He has written several novels, as well as one of my favorite books about writing, *On Writing*. If *Stephen King* needs time to write, then so do I. And so do students!

Whenever I talk or write about writing instruction, I find myself using analogies, and many of them involve sports. In any sport, practice is necessary. Expanding the idea of practice, it's necessary for any pursuit or activity. In a different study, another one of Graham et al.'s (2018) key recommendations for effective writing instruction involves providing *daily* time for students to write with time allocated for explicit instruction, as well as independent application. Graves also emphasized the importance of time spent writing. According to Graves, at least four days per week of time dedicated to writing instruction is necessary for students to enjoy writing and contribute to their personal development as learners (Graves, n.d.a).

BELIEF 4: WRITERS NEED A COMMUNITY

Teachers who write set the stage for a writing community, but a community also consists of co-learners and thoughtful responders. I love to listen to students collaborate about their pieces; sometimes they co-create, and other times they respond with questions, compliments, and suggestions. Writing can be an act of vulnerability, since not every writer knows what to say, how to say it, and what the response could be. While there are a variety of potential audiences for writers, a community provides an organic first audience, and with supports and structures, that community can become a place where writers take risks, experimenting, analyzing, and celebrating the power of their written pieces.

These beliefs rest on the shoulders and thinking of many leaders in the education field who have shaped my development as a writing teacher, and at some point, I may change or add to them. However, I keep coming back to these four beliefs time and time again, year after year.

WHY IS TEACHING WRITING DIFFERENT TODAY?

Before thinking about the differences between teaching writing today and at any other time, it's important to remember that the goal of writing instruction, regardless of time frame and context, is to empower students to use language with precision and flexibility so that they can communicate their ideas, beliefs, knowledge, and stories. That purpose has not changed, and I don't foresee it ever changing. The ability to communicate empowers everyone across the domains of their lives—personally, emotionally, professionally, and civically. Keeping that goal as a beacon and north star clarifies how to analyze and select the strategies, resources, and technology that evolve and are invented in a rapidly changing environment.

Returning to Graham's recommendations, teaching students to become fluent with handwriting, spelling, sentence construction, typing, and word processing are critical. With less cognitive demand required for basic writing skills, students can use more energy for creating and developing ideas. Perhaps more than any other impact, the availability and wide usage of technology have changed the teaching of writing because technology has the power to make some of those basic writing skills more accessible to students. For example, let's think about revision and how it relates to teaching writing in today's classrooms. Young students may need paper strips to add ideas or you may need to teach them how to use asterisks and arrows, but once students learn to use a keyboard, revision can happen without the worry of where to fit it in.

I graduated from high school in the mid-eighties, and my graduation present was a typewriter that could delete several characters that I didn't want. Even so, I didn't like using that function because the erasing tape was so expensive! Before the typewriter, my father used to read my handwritten high school essays in the morning. (To this day, I do not know what possessed me to show him those essays since some of the biggest fights I can remember happened because he used a pen on my final copy.) I didn't even always agree with what he perceived as mistakes. I allowed myself only one to two corrections per page, so at the least, my father's corrections meant I'd have to rewrite the entire page and possibly more. I often wonder how those mornings would have gone if we could have copied, pasted, and deleted text without having to redo the entire piece.

The idea of revising a writing piece may not overwhelm writers as much when change doesn't involve rewriting pages by hand, and that's a good thing. However, as is the case with so much technology, there's another not-so-positive side. Revising within an online platform means the writer's process becomes less visible.

When students cross out, add asterisks and carats, and write in margins or at different parts of paper pages, their thinking and their process has a trail; many times it's easier to teach when that sort of trail exists. Because of the less visible trail on devices, students' understanding and ability to verbalize their steps, strengths, and struggles as writers are even more important so they can share them with teachers, and instruction can be more targeted on what is helpful for students.

Final products are important for writing, and in this book, you will read about the tension between process and product, an important distinction for writing teachers to consider throughout their work with students. Word processing has impacted the products that students are able to create, and using a keyboard or a device facilitates the creation of an easier-to-read end piece that looks more like texts students are accustomed to reading (MacArthur, 2000). However, when the emphasis is on a product and not on the learning that happens along the way, students may become intimidated by the process of writing itself. There is a constant balance that teeters and shifts of nudging students to learn and develop, as opposed to pushing students to create a piece of writing that goes out into the world and can be easily and respectfully accessed by an audience. A way to find the balance when you find yourself teetering is to remember that not all pieces need to be all things.

TECHNOLOGY HAS CHANGED THE STUDENT WRITING EXPERIENCE

The basic premise of writing to communicate ideas was true before the influx of computers and digital opportunities, and it remains true today. However, as computers and devices become more and more available to students, writing instruction has changed. At this time, the evidence is mixed regarding whether student writing improves based on the platform of pen to paper or keyboarding (Spilling et al., 2021), and it could be that the answer varies from student to student. The important thing to realize is that writing involves the integration of many attributes and skills, from physical strength to fine motor to extensive cognitive ones.

When I work with young writers, writers who are still using paper and haven't yet learned to keyboard, I teach them early on not to erase. "Just use a single line to cross out," I tell them. That way, they spend less time erasing and writing, erasing and writing, and also, I have access to their process as writers. What decisions did they make about revision? What did they change and why?

The trail that these young writers leave provides me with insights into their process as writers, and those understandings help me teach them more effectively. Online mediums and digital platforms complicate this process. I can ask students to track changes, and with some digital platforms, I can see a history of revisions. I can coach students to ignore computer-based suggestions and potentially distracting red lines, but I can't see the process the way I can when it's on paper, and I can't always know that students aren't distracted by technology's attempts to be helpful. As is the case with so many things in both writing instruction and life, there's a balance to find between how technology helps and how it hinders. Instruction may sometimes focus on when it's easier for students to create on paper as opposed to on a screen. At what point should a piece be printed as a hard copy and suggestions made in the margin with a pen? Those answers will differ from student to student and from piece to piece, and the search for these answers adds to the complexity of writing instruction.

In addition to facilitating the revision process, technology offers many alternatives to the accurate spelling of words. Spellcheck programs have gotten better and better, which also has pros and cons when it comes to writing instruction. On the one hand, this automation potentially allows students to pay more attention to the content of their work, as opposed to mechanics that are more easily corrected by a teacher or other reader. On the other hand, at what point should students know how to spell high-frequency words? Today's writing instruction requires teachers to contemplate that balance constantly. There are a few words that I always struggle to spell (parallelism, embarrassment, parentheses), and I am grateful for the red lines that indicate there's a problem or even the instant correction. However, if those corrections happened constantly, my ability to concentrate on content and composition would decrease because of the distractions.

Dictation is another complication for current writing instruction. "Use talk to text" is a suggestion I hear in many intervention meetings. Yes, many students can talk faster than they write, and they have access to programs and apps that can transcribe their words. However, as a friend who bakes amazing cookies reminds me, the product will be only as good as the ingredients. If you're putting not-good stuff in, you'll get not-good stuff out. Dictation has the potential to frustrate many students because they might not be able to speak clearly, they might not initiate the process with organized thoughts, or they might not consider the conventions and punctuation their writing needs to include to be created for users to access and read.

One of my yoga teacher's mantras is that not every body is everybody. I like to transfer that to writing instruction: Not every writer needs the same skills, lesson, or focus. Maybe one student struggles with letter formation but has no problem finding letters on a keyboard; that student may well compose more effectively using a device. Technology has the power to provide access and pathways for some students that were nonexistent before the wide use and availability of computers and personal devices. These discrepancies, differences, and decisions impact writing instruction.

Within all these concepts, these questions remain at the heart of writing instruction: How well are students able to communicate their ideas? Can they do it independently? Are the tools that are available to them in classrooms also available to them outside of the classrooms? Will the instruction and system you offer them help or hinder them in the future? No matter when you read this book, no matter what technology is available in the world and in your classroom, hold on to your key beliefs about your end goals for students as writers. You want to empower those students to communicate their ideas with the world, and every tool, resource, and strategy should aim at that ultimate goal.

How Does Writing Instruction Overlap With Universal Design for Learning (UDL)?

Given the development of technology and the continuing research that exists about learning, more possibilities exist for writers, as well as more knowledge about how the process develops. Universal Design for Learning (UDL) provides guidelines with a set of concrete suggestions for any discipline or domain that "ensure that all learners can access and participate in meaningful, challenging learning opportunities" (CAST, n.d.). Within three broad categories of engagement, representation, and action and expression, UDL provides guidelines for the why, what, and how of learning. These categories apply directly to writing instruction. As you read this book, consider the various reasons you provide for developing writers to create pieces. This consideration folds into one of my guiding beliefs about purpose and audience. Technology has expanded the possibilities for both what writers create and the tools and resources they have available for them.

While there is much more to know and understand about UDL—and I recommend spending time exploring and familiarizing yourself with UDL for all content areas—remembering the three pillars of engagement, representation, and action and expression is helpful for considering and creating modifications that open pathways for all writers in your classroom.

For more about UDL, go to cast.org.

EQUITY MUST BE AT THE CENTER

Graham's recommendations, combined with UDL and a clear belief set, create a trajectory aimed at equity, critical in every aspect of curriculum and instruction. Throughout this book, when I address equity, I lean on the definition and description created by the National Equity Project (n.d.): *Educational equity means that each child receives what they need to develop to their full academic and social potential.*

Because the process of writing is complex, requiring both precursive skills and the integration of developing ones, instruction is complex, and there are many ways to provide it so that everyone meets their potential. In *The Responsive Writing Teacher*, Kelsey Sorum and I (2021) present four domains to consider across all components of writing instruction: academic, linguistic, cultural, and social-emotional. Knowing the writers in your classroom across each domain will help you plan for and provide equitable instruction.

When considering the academic domain, it is critical to gather information, plan, and provide resources for where students are functioning when it comes to skills and knowledge. Teaching concepts that require extensive scaffolding and support reinforces students' belief that writing is beyond their realm of possibility, a message that does not lead to meeting academic potential. Rigorous curriculum and high expectations must be combined with pathways of possibilities and embedded experiences for success and agency.

Linguistic responsiveness is the second domain for writing teachers to pay close attention to. As Ludwig Wittgenstein (1921/2010), an Austrian philosopher, wrote, "the limits of my language mean the limits of my world." In other words, students' abilities to process and produce language impact their writing ability, and how we plan and provide for language development helps or hinders students from meeting their full potential.

Just as it's possible to respond to and act on students' academic and linguistic abilities, understanding and responding to cultural and social-emotional aspects of their lives send strong messages regarding what you value about them. Additionally, deepening your understanding of who students are, what matters to them, and how they learn opens possibilities for topics, learning pathways, and environmental priorities. All these factors expand the trajectory of meeting potential, both academically and socially.

Zaretta Hammond (2021) expands the concept of equity with three distinct dimensions of equity. She distinguishes between *multicultural education* with a focus on celebrating diversity; *social justice education*, which exposes the experiences of the social-political contexts of students; and *culturally responsive education*, which improves the learning capacity of historically marginalized students. Writing instruction has the power to provide straightforward access to multiculturalism and social justice by providing students with a range of mentor texts and choices of topics that have personal meaning for them. Furthermore, writing is a mechanism for activism and social justice. The more students understand, learn, and utilize the power of writing to create differences in the world, the more engagement, purpose, and passion they will have for their own agency and process.

The more impactful differences on students' learning and achievement when it comes to equity are entangled within students' ability to accept and embrace agency and self-directed learning. The trajectory of this book moves from the consideration of your environment to the curriculum to instruction and assessment, so that in the final chapter, you can grapple with how all those components can work together beneath the all-important umbrella of student agency. As your emphasis shifts to student-directedness and agency, so does students' ability to improve their own cognitive development and writing skills. As Hammond (2021) writes, "Our ultimate goal is to design learning so students become self-aware and self-directed as learners. Then they can grow their smarts and expand their intellectual capacity." It is this expansion that leads to high levels of learning for all students—the ultimate goal of equity in education.

HOW DOES THIS BOOK HELP?

The five chapters of this book encompass the environment, the curriculum, instructional practices, assessment, and ways to provide agency to students. Curating many of the questions I have heard during my time as a writing teacher and specialist, I have created questions that aim at those topics. Sometimes my own writing and teaching experiences have helped me answer them, sometimes I've talked to colleagues I admire, and other times I've culled through research. The overarching questions, which serve as chapter titles, are as follows:

1. How Do I Build and Maintain a Writing Community?
2. What Should Students Know and Be Able to Do as Writers?
3. What Are Key Instructional Practices to Know and Use?
4. How Do I Use Assessment for Students' Benefit?
5. How Do I Shift Agency From Teacher to Students in the Writing Classroom?

These questions aim to address the instructional core—curriculum, instruction, and assessment—while providing equity and agency for all students. You will find sidebar notes throughout the text that provide explanations and windows into my interior debates and decision-making as I work with writers. You will also find lists of additional resources because this book is designed to help you get going and then check in with yourself.

The body of work about writing instruction is enormous, and people contribute to it daily. I am grateful for the ideas and contributions of the many educators in my own district who grapple and reflect to inspire students to write. My colleagues at Two Writing Teachers also influence my understanding of how to teach writing well. And all our work stands on the shoulders of great writing instructors, including Donald Graves, Steve Graham, Lucy Calkins, Ruth Culham, Frank Smith, Zaretta Hammond, and many more.

WHOM IS THIS BOOK FOR?

While I hope this book helps anyone new to teaching writing, I also hope that it helps *anyone* who would like more confidence in teaching writing! Various programs exist, whether they are unit-based, workshop-based, or based on purchased scripts and resources. Across the country, students experience a wide variety of curriculum, instruction, lessons, activities, and experiences when it comes to writing instruction. Ultimately, the goal of any writing instruction, though, should be to develop students who can identify and communicate their ideas, stories, and knowledge. If you work with students who are at any stage of their writing lives, you may find resources and strategies in this book that inspire you.

The challenge of distilling practices into five prioritized ideas has led to the clear articulation of what has worked for me over the years of teaching writing to elementary students. At times, you may find overlap or redundancy, and that may be because writing instruction is recursive and nonlinear. Each of the first four chapters builds to the fifth chapter, where the focus is on the key shift from teacher-driven learning to student-driven learning. Research shows that the more students develop agency for themselves as writers, the higher the rates of growth and learning you're likely to see (Zeiser, Scholz, & Cirks, 2018).

If you are a teacher in the early part of your career using this book as you develop your practices, you may find satisfaction and inspiration in thinking about how you set up your systems and structures, what you teach, how you teach, how you measure, and how you empower and center students.

More experienced teachers may find in this book validation for your practices. You may also find the language or explanation to clarify practices for others who work with you, co-teaching or supporting writers in their classrooms. It could be that the fifth chapter, which focuses on agency, is a starting place for experienced teachers who are looking to provide more opportunities for students to take charge of their own learning.

For those of you who observe and evaluate writing instruction, this book can provide look-fors and listen-fors. It may help you sharpen your lens for noticing environments that support learners, and maybe you'll find opportunities for providing feedback that builds confidence and grows practice. Classroom teachers face a wide range of writers, and the more you can offer ideas about instructional strategies, the better for all those writers.

Writing coaches and district curriculum specialists can use this book to develop common vocabulary and practices within the classrooms you support. You may also consider how to communicate classroom instructional practices that meet the various needs and learning opportunities for the wide variety of writers in classrooms, ideas that comprise Chapter 3. Many opportunities exist for assessment in writing classrooms, and maybe Chapter 4 becomes a focus area when meetings arise for individual students of concern.

HOW SHOULD YOU USE THIS BOOK?

In my experience, the most effective teachers of writing are in a constant state of reflection and development. Their lessons are never the same, their strategies evolve, and their resources reflect and respond to the students who are in their classrooms. Just as the writing process is not linear, neither is writing instruction. And this book honors that nonlinear process!

Writing is recursive, or looped in a way that allows each phase of writing to repeat. Meehan and Sorum (2021) share their writing processes in *The Responsive Writing Teacher*, showing and explaining how writers move back and forth between steps within their writing processes. Each step feeds into another step, possibly one that has already been experienced with the same writing piece. Drafting may lead to the need for more research and fact-finding. Revision may send writers back to reconsider their plan. Just as the writing process is recursive, so is writing instruction. As you learn and weave new practices and ideas into your practice, you may want to return to other related practices and ideas as well. Use this book in a way that brings you back to the particular point you need at the time you need it.

Maybe you'll want to read this book cover to cover the first time. If you do, think about the flow as setting up to teach, figuring out what to teach and how to teach it, and then taking into consideration how to know that students are learning and benefiting from your instruction. Throughout it all, continue to ask yourself, how do I promote student agency?

Or maybe you'll think to yourself, *okay, I'm getting the idea of instructional practices, so how can I make sure my environment supports them?* With that question, you might want to return to Chapter 1.

And maybe you're feeling like all the parts are coming together, and you want to work on shifting agency in your writing classroom. In that case, start with Chapter 5.

Because the book centers on questions, you might find questions you have or didn't know you have but have now—exploring some of those answers and explanations is another way you might use this book.

My hope is that this book becomes a coach by your side as you develop your own practice of writing instruction. No matter where you are in that practice, there's room to reflect and grow, especially as resources and technology continue to evolve and improve the opportunities for students to learn.

chapter ONE

HOW DO I BUILD AND MAINTAIN A WRITING COMMUNITY?

Dia, a third-grader, loved cupcakes, and she wrote an opinion piece about a local bakery. Her teacher did a little sleuthing, found the bakery's contact information, and emailed the piece. Dia's piece became the featured Instagram post for the Cupcake Gypsy, and then, to the excitement of her classmates, the owner delivered two-dozen individually wrapped cupcakes to their classroom get-together. What an identity Dia established for herself as a writer!

It's easy to spot the elements of purpose, play, and passion in this classroom example. Not every writing community will have the gift of fresh cupcakes from a local bakery as the byproduct of someone's opinion writing, but the more you establish community, purpose, and passion in your classroom, the more potential for authenticity in writing lives and high levels of learning and achievement. Cupcake appreciation is the tip of the iceberg when it comes to the power of possibilities that writing creates.

Figure 1.1 Dia was excited that her writing led to cupcakes for her entire class.

Throughout this chapter, think about how to help students establish writing identities and build and sustain a community where students experience a world as full of possibilities for entertaining, informing, and arguing.

This chapter answers the following questions:

- ☐ **How do I build a writing community with predictable structures and accessible resources?**
- ☐ **How do I get to know individual students as people and as writers?**
- ☐ **What are some systems and structures of a writing community?**
- ☐ **How do I engage and communicate with families/caregivers?**
- ☐ **What resources should I have available to support students' independence?**
- ☐ **How do I establish a risk-taking environment that feels safe, supportive, and joyful?**
- ☐ **How do we celebrate progress as a community?**
- ☐ **How do I communicate the importance, power, and joy that writing brings?**

As you read this chapter, I encourage you to think about your own writing life and ways to develop it, as well as the feeling you want all students to have as writers in your classroom. I also encourage you to think about the environment you and your students create for them to take risks, utilize resources, and learn at high levels.

How Do I Build a Writing Community With Predictable Structures and Accessible Resources?

A historic definition of community may imply that people are living in the same place. However, when thinking about a writing community, the definition is more abstract and involves more than a zip code. Instead of sharing a neighborhood, a writing community shares a common space, language, systems, and set of beliefs. Additionally, members of a writing community care about each other and work toward related goals.

Because of these communal elements, it's critical to establish an environment with systems and structures that students know, understand, and expect. That way, the community nurtures and strengthens the individuals within it. Taking the time to consider and decide on these concepts will have a positive impact on your writing community throughout the year, emphasizing that all members of the community see themselves as writers.

KNOW YOUR OWN IDENTITY AS A WRITER

In the introduction, I shared some foundational beliefs about what writers need, and one of those needs is a teacher who writes. Because you are the lead writer and the person students look to as their example, it's important that you have and know your identity as a writer. Remember that weeklong writing workshop mentioned in the introduction? One of the first things the leaders had us do was head into town and buy a writer's notebook. My colleague, Anne, and I thought we were attending the workshop to deepen our knowledge of writing instruction, and we learned that one of the most important first steps we could do was to write and get to know ourselves as writers. Throughout the week, we worked in our notebooks, exploring our own comforts and discomforts with writing. Anne and I discovered that we had different identities; she created descriptions and moods through words while I developed plots. Anne's plots were developed through her scenes, while my descriptions happened as a result of revision.

Our reflections have stayed with me throughout my writing life, even as my identity as a writer has changed and developed. I pay attention to what is easy for me, as well as what challenges me. I pay attention to what I do when challenges arise, and I pay attention to the environment and variables that support my most productive writing moments.

It's easier for many classroom teachers to think of themselves as a reader than it is to think of themselves as a writer. Somehow, in many minds, to identify as a writer involves readership and publication. But does it? Writing takes on many forms: list-making, report cards, emails, texts, thank-you notes, completion of forms, and so on. Take a moment and consider how many written messages you create on any given day. You are a writer!

As you write, it's important to pay attention to your own identity, especially as you try to write texts like the ones you expect students to write. Those texts serve as mentors or demonstration texts, and they also communicate to students that you are a writer as well. Some questions that you might consider as you develop your own writing identity include, but aren't limited to:

- When do I write and for what purposes?
- What aspects of writing are hard for me, and what makes them easier?
- What helps me get started with a writing project?
- Where and when am I the most productive as a writer?
- Is there a genre I feel most comfortable with?
- Are there topics I return to over and over?
- How important is choice to me?
- How much do I consider my audience?

 Equity and Access

Within the classroom writing community, it's important for students to see your insecurities as a writer. Writing is a vulnerable process, and most professional and published writers will share their self-doubt. Within the community, writers will grow when the community celebrates process and progress, emphasizes the setting and sharing of goals, and normalizes imperfection. Additionally, when the community values process and progress, students feel safer taking risks, which leads to more culturally relevant experiences and greater equity for all students. Competence leads to confidence, which leads to risk-taking and learning. As you learn about writing identities, you can zero in on positive experiences and places of perceived strengths, places that lead to a willingness and commitment to learn.

The more you understand and can explain your identity as a writer, the more you'll be able to teach students to identify theirs. You can't necessarily have all optimal conditions met in a writing classroom of so many people—my best writing time is early in the morning when it's super quiet and my coffee is fresh!—but you can work to know and understand differences and preferences.

ESTABLISH AND COMMUNICATE YOUR FOUNDATIONAL BELIEFS ABOUT WRITING

When you know your own identity as a writer, it becomes easier to establish and then communicate foundational beliefs about writing. What do you believe about writing? Are you able to say this? A shared belief set is a powerful structure to have in place for developing any kind of community. When you have one, you can communicate it to students and also to the people at home who are interested in the students' writing lives. In the introduction, I shared my beliefs about what students need as writers: choice, a teacher who writes, and time to write. Additionally, I maintain a belief set about what my instruction should include. This set evolves more than my core beliefs, but for the time being, it includes:

- My teaching should be transferable for future pieces. If I am teaching or correcting too much, then my focus is on a singular piece of writing and I may be creating *dependent* writers as opposed to *independent* writers.

- Good writing does not have to be perfect writing. Sometimes the quest for perfect gets in the way of the process, and I want writers to take risks and try out ideas with bravery.
- Envisioning an audience is powerful but not necessary. Writers create pieces for different reasons. Sometimes those reasons lend themselves to a specific audience, and sometimes those reasons may be personal. In either case, there is validity and importance for writing.
- Writers benefit from resources. Not everyone needs the same thing at the same time, but sample writing, mentor texts, charts, and checklists are important resources to have available for writers of all levels.

Clear belief sets about writing will ground your thinking as you communicate with students, colleagues, and caregivers. It's worth taking the time to think about your beliefs, write them, and refer to them. You're also free to revise them as you develop your identity as a writing teacher.

Notes

How Do I Get to Know Individual Students as People and as Writers?

My daughters have all graduated from high school, and all four of them agree that their best teachers, the ones who inspired them the most, were teachers who asked, knew, and cared about their personal lives. Knowing students matters!

KNOW STUDENTS AS PEOPLE FIRST

You will come across students who say they have nothing to write. Many times. One of your best moves is to coach them to think about what matters to them. Fourth-grader Ronan sat through several opinion writing sessions without writing much until his teacher asked me how to help. She watched a video of a conference with him, and she couldn't believe how much time I spent talking about what he does—and not about writing. "I want a topic that matters to him," I explained. That day, his teacher made it her priority to listen to Ronan and his friends at recess, and they were arguing over sports cars. His attitude toward writing took a dramatic shift when it involved the merits of Teslas as opposed to Maseratis.

Knowing students as individuals will empower you to lead them to find the moments of meaning within their own lives. What do they do when they go home from school? What brings them joy? What makes them angry? Who are the important people in their lives, as well as their favorite places and things to do? What do they watch on screens? What do they listen to from speakers? When you know the answers to these questions and more, you will be able to ask questions and make suggestions that lead to stories and writing topics. In *The Responsive Writing Teacher*, Meehan and Sorum (2021) provide a tool (Figure 1.2) you can use to ensure that you are thinking about the interests of students. You can access it on the companion website, resources.corwin.com/answerselementarywriting.

This interest inventory is one way to create a system and structure for knowing students, but there are many additional ways. The focus should be on a stance of curiosity and appreciation for the personal and learning lives of all students.

SHARE YOUR OWN PERSONAL IDENTITY

Identity webs are powerful for sharing information about you and your life with students. If you haven't made one, I highly recommend taking the time (maybe even right now!) and creating one.

The Facing Hard History website, as well as Sara K. Ahmed's (2018) book, *Being the Change*, provides questions to consider as you design your own identity web.

- Who am I?
- What are my family connections?
- What do I love?
- What are key events that have impacted me?

- What do I do every day?
- What words might others use to describe you that you might or might not use to describe yourself?

Figure 1.2 Collecting information about students is important for building the classroom community.

COLLECTING INFORMATION ABOUT STUDENT INTERESTS

STUDENTS *(List all students in your classroom; use multiple sheets if necessary.)*	INTERESTS **Notice:** books read, topics of writing, topics of drawings, topics of conversations, choices at playtime or recess **Might include:** family members, pets, animals, music, TV shows or movies, sports, hobbies, places, toys, family traditions, holidays		

Source: Meehan & Sorum (2021).

Figure 1.3 My identity web serves as a model for others, both students and teachers.

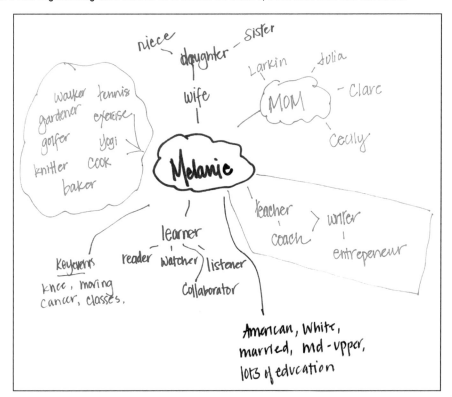

When you share aspects of your identity, students are much more apt to share. Additionally, your identity web provides a model and mentor for students. Remember that one of my core beliefs is that teachers should write. You will be a more effective teacher of identity webs if you have experienced the creation of your own!

When you make the effort to get to know students on a personal level, that effort signifies that you care about them. People will take risks and try new things when they feel cared about, and writing can be a vulnerable process that goes better when people feel safe. Identity webs provide important insights into the lives and priorities of students. What students choose to share—and also what they choose *not* to share—will help you build connections and guide them to meaningful writing throughout the year.

Great Resources

- Sara K. Ahmed (2018) offers various ways to get to know students as people in her book, *Being the Change*. One idea is to make sure that you can associate both nouns and adjectives with all students. Who are the important people in their lives? What are their favorite activities? Knowing these people and activities becomes both the foundation of trust and of topics for writing.

- Kathleen Sokoloski (2021) is a third-grade teacher in New York with many strategies for getting to know students, even before she meets them. Before the start of school, she creates a Flipgrid to introduce herself and invites students to do the same.

- FacingHistory.org, a website and resource for teaching students about the past to create more equity in the future, describes identity webs as tools for considering the many factors that shape who we are, not only as individuals but also as community members. If you haven't ever tried making an identity web, you might consider making one now. As an example, I am offering my most recent one, one that I made as a mentor for students who were participating in a virtual writing class.

KNOW STUDENTS AS WRITERS

Meehan and Sorum (2021) present four domains for knowing students. The concepts referenced above address the cultural and social-emotional domains of students as writers. It's also important to learn about them as writers, considering more of the academic and linguistic domains. The academic domain focuses on what students know and are able to do as writers when it comes to content-related skills and the writing process, while the linguistic domain addresses language processing skills.

Figure 1.4 Thinking about different domains reminds teachers to consider various dimensions of students' identities.

Academic Responsiveness ↓	Linguistic Responsiveness ↓	Cultural Responsiveness ↓	Social-Emotional Responsiveness ↓
Collect information about . . .			
Students' proficiency with content-related skills Writing-related behaviors as students engage in a writing process	Students' home language(s), speaking and processing skills, language use, and vocabulary development	The cultural and social identities of students	Student interests within and outside of school The social-emotional tendencies of students in relation to writing

Source: Meehan & Sorum (2021).

Knowing, understanding, and considering these domains will deepen the sense of community and the impact of instruction throughout the year.

In *Feedback That Moves Writers Forward*, Patty McGee (2017) identifies several reasons people write with correlating suggestions about identity. She reminds readers that students write to entertain, or figure out feelings, or persuade. Expanding on the choices and different experiences writers may face and prefer, they could prefer expressing themselves or planning through pictures, and maybe they would rather use a keyboard than a pen and paper. Coppola (2019) and Stockman (2021) also broaden the understanding of what writing and communication can look like and involve. All these reasons, choices, and preferences for writing are foundational for writing identities.

In addition to establishing these choices and principles of writing in your classroom, it's important to build on those foundations by inviting students to share their past experiences as writers. I like to ask students to create a timeline of their own writing lives. This activity is potentially more robust for older students than it is for primary ones, but even young children can draw and label important moments in their writing lives.

Equity and Access

Timelines relate to equity because they provide lenses into where, how, and why writers have felt success and where, when, and why they have also struggled or felt incompetent. When you know this information, then you can work to create more positive experiences for writers in your classrooms, which leads to higher levels of learning.

I begin with my own, sharing the authentic writing experiences I can remember having as a child, including everything from learning to follow dots that created letters to winning a poetry contest. Then I ask students to create their own timeline, leaning into questions such as:

- When do you remember feeling proud of your writing?
- What compliment(s) have you received?
- What are some of the pieces of writing you can remember creating?
- When do you remember struggling? What happened?
- What are some of the positive memories you have of writing? What are some negative ones?
- When have you written outside of the classroom?

  - Letters?
  - Lists?
  - Notes?

Figure 1.5 A writing timeline provides teachers and students with insights into their identities as writers.

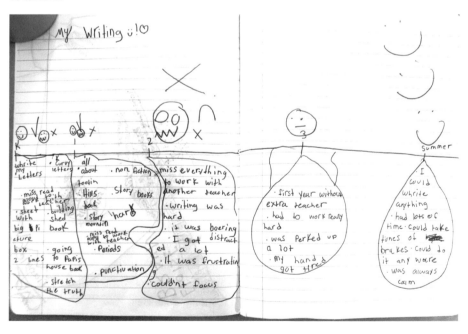

I also ask students to consider what they are good at as writers, as well as what are growth areas for them. Typically, when I ask students to first consider what they are good at, their initial response encompasses conventions, neatness, and spelling. These responses invite conversation with students about what else good writing entails. Often, less confident writers will light up when they recognize that effective writers do much more. Effective writers pay attention to their world, notice details, think of ideas, plan, and figure out ways to relay their messages. These conversations and realizations invite writers into the community of writers that may have previously felt exclusive and intimidating.

Figure 1.6 Students can think about what they are good at, as well as what they are working on as writers.

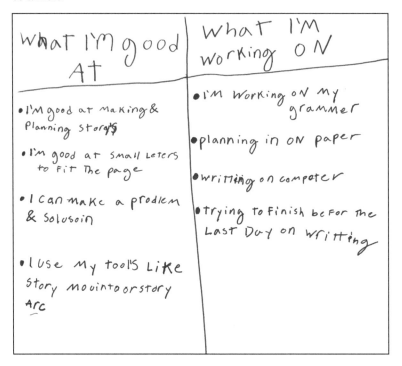

Just as students appreciate your knowing them as people, they also appreciate being known as writers. Moreover, most students will not have thought about themselves as writers before, considering the idea of "I'm the kind of writer who . . ." The more they understand that their experiences are shared experiences that other writers have, the more validation they have as writers.

Agency and Identity

When students make identity maps and timelines, they share key parts of their lives. As they create timelines, they become more reflective about their own writing lives and identities. These experiences help you guide them toward topics, goal-setting, and understanding of their learning processes.

ESTABLISH THE COMMUNITY
OF A GROUP OF WRITERS

> Writing is a social act. If social actions are to work, then the establishment of a community is essential. A highly predictable classroom is required if children are to learn to take responsibility and become a community of learners who help each other. Writing is an unpredictable act requiring predictable classrooms both in structure and response. (Graves, n.d.a)

Donald Graves was a leader in literacy education, and his research and writing led to the transformation of writing instruction in many elementary classrooms. Through several books, articles, interviews, and presentations, Graves brought a workshop-like element to the writing lives of children so that their writing experiences became based more on their needs and interests. While his work led to more authenticity to the writing lives of children, it also led to more unpredictability within the writing process. Authentic writing is not predictable, as he wrote in the above quote. Authentic writing is messy, unique, and unchartered. There is not a correct response or right answer when it comes to authentic writing. Instead, it demands unscripted response and reaction. Because of the unpredictability that the process guarantees, the establishment of systems and structures becomes that much more important to the community of writers.

Thinking about the social aspect of writing increases the urgency of establishing a community where writers know and appreciate each other. Students need to learn to talk and listen to each other to respond and react to each other's writing. Spend time creating the knowledge of who you all are together in the classroom you share for the year. I love Kathleen Sokoloski's (2021) idea to create a nonrhyming poem or song that tells about the learners:

We are Room ____.

We are readers, writers, and thinkers.

We love poetry, fantasy, and mystery.

We love Jason Reynolds, Kate DiCamillo, and Mary Pope Osborne.

We are Room ____.

A poem like this one could continue with various stanzas about various elements of the overall community. Maybe a stanza about favorite activities, family situations, or approaches to challenges. It could even become a song, and it is also a piece of writing that could evolve throughout the year, continually and constantly serving as a beacon for the importance of revision.

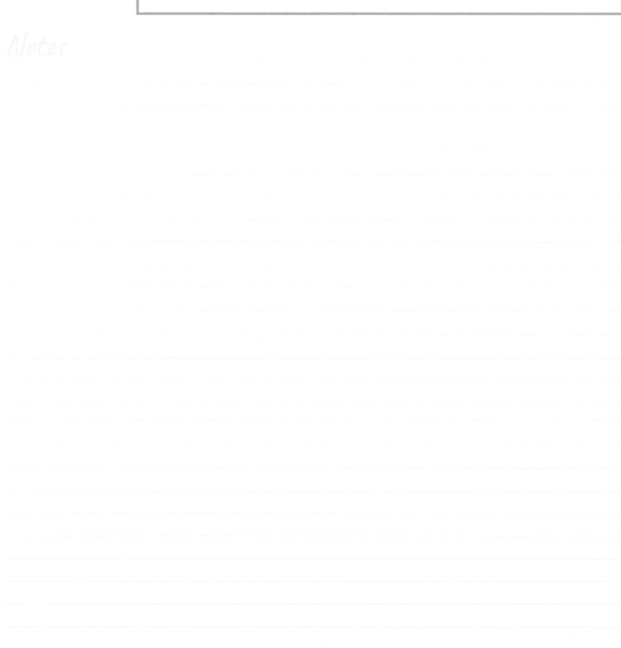

Additional Questions to Consider Within a Writing Community

While it's great to establish guidelines for a writing community within the first few weeks of school, you can consider the following questions with students at any time:

- How much time do writers need to think, plan, compose, and share?
- What type of space do I prefer to work in?
- What is and is not an acceptable noise level during writing time?
- Who is my audience? Who do I choose to share with? Why do I share my work?
- What tools help best create my message?

Notes

What Are Some Systems and Structures of a Writing Community?

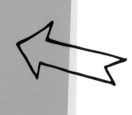

As is the case with any community, a writing community thrives on systems and structures that all community members understand. As you consider some of these elements, think also about how students can have ownership of their development.

A COMMON LANGUAGE

As you establish your classroom's writing community, you will want to consider the terms and common language you want students to know and understand. In Chapter 3, you will read more about whole group instruction and the opportunities for inquiry lessons, as well as more about what the terms below mean and how they relate to instruction. That being said, language is a critical component of a community, and key terms could be a wonderful inquiry lesson: *What words and ideas do we all need to know for writing class to go well?* I envision this lesson to be about essential elements, materials, and processes in a writing classroom, including but not limited to:

- Writer's notebooks: Keeping places for ideas, plans, strategies, and more
- Charts: Visual representations of the learning that's happening
- Mentor texts: Books and other texts that inspire writers with craft moves and ideas they can duplicate
- Planning: Part of the writing process that helps writers know and remember what will be included in their pieces
- Drafting: The writing of a piece itself, to be done outside of the notebook
- Revising: The process of adding and eliminating text to make it stronger and clearer for readers
- Editing: The adding of punctuation, capitalization, and spelling to make it easier for an audience to read

You could create a chart along the lines of Figure 1.7, on the next page.

What Are Some Systems and Structures of a Writing Community?

23

Figure 1.7 A common vocabulary helps communities function at high levels.

The responses to this question should vary from class to class, grade to grade, and teacher to teacher, recognizing the importance and value of a shared language among community members.

COMMON AND INDIVIDUAL GOALS

Students should understand what they are working on, and they should have systems and structures for expressing their goals. Not everyone will be working on the same thing at the same time—that undermines the importance of independence and choice. You will want to establish and cultivate a community of goal-setters, a mindset that will benefit all content areas, and not just writing.

How do we push students to think beyond the goals that they score on fields or in rinks, and toward the goals they can set for themselves within more academic settings?

An important starting point for students at all levels across all content areas is to teach them about goals, and the following questions provide entry points into important conversations:

- What is a goal?
- What inspires goal-setters?
- What gets in the way of goal-setters?
- How do we decide on goals?

The answers to these questions vary for experienced goal-setters and brand-new ones. Some people don't like to announce goals. Others need a daily reminder. Some people thrive with goal partners, and other people may need more reinforcement along their goal-achieving pathway. To make the answers to these questions even more complicated, goal-setting patterns should evolve, as people learn about themselves and develop growth mindsets. As comfort levels grow in the goal-setting process, public goal-setting may become inspiring instead of uncomfortable.

Agency and Identity

Goal-setting is a way to build agency for learners. When students decide on, know and understand, and make a plan for their own learning, you are much more likely to see growth!

Because of the variation in goal-achieving strategies and techniques, you may want various ways to present them to students. Here are a few that you could incorporate into writing instruction.

- **Develop a repertoire of questions that keeps the responsibility for learning with the student.**

  - What are you working on?
  - What is your goal as a learner for this work?
  - What strategies are you using to help with this goal?
  - What strategies would you like to work on to help with this goal?

  Feel free to develop others, but keep using the language of setting goals, developing strategies, and working on techniques. Soon, you will find your students speaking naturally about their goals and strategies.

- **Create checklists that encourage learning.** I love the checklists that are included in *Writing Pathways* by Lucy Calkins (2014) for many reasons, but an important reason has to do with the columns for "starting to" and "not yet." These phrases imply that these skills will develop, but learners must work at them. The important trick is to get students to evaluate their work reflectively and see the power in setting targets and goals. We shouldn't have all our checks in the yes column if we are really learning!

- **Involve students in their selection of daily learning.** Teachers I work with set up seminars for students, and students can sign up or register for them. Seminar sign-ups help manage small group instruction (more on that in Chapters 3 and 5), and they also inherently involve students in goal-setting and ownership of their learning lives.

Figure 1.8 When students sign up for seminars, it builds their goal-setting mindsets.

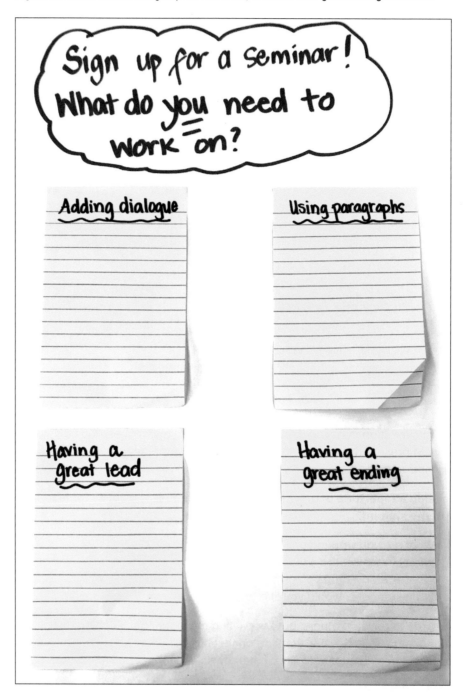

- **Nurture the habit of leaving goal cards with students when you confer with them.** In my toolkit, I keep blank 3 × 5 cards. Whenever I work with a student, I leave a card. (More on this in Chapter 3.) That way, *everyone* knows what that student is working on, including and especially the student. These cards serve as a teaching point and as a strategy card for the goals of the individual student.

My most important and impactful learning moments have all involved goals. Celebrate the accomplishments of students, help them understand all they have learned and achieved, and then keep nudging them to set goals that focus on their writing lives.

ROUTINES

Many exercise classes have a structure they follow, and different instructors may vary it. Regular participants expect a routine or structure, even if it changes a bit from time to time or instructor to instructor. And most participants would express a comfort in their expectations. "This is the part when . . ." is a phrase that grounds people and invites them to think less about what will come next and more about what they are working on at that given moment.

Taking the time to establish routines, roles, and responsibilities provides security and stability for the writing community. In Chapter 3, I talk extensively about the roles and responsibilities of both teachers and students during writing instruction. I also talk more about materials and resources in that chapter as they relate to instruction, but they also relate to the environment. That being said, there are routines pertaining to the environment and the materials that you'll use and want to establish. Some routines may include, but aren't limited to:

- What paper do students use, and how and where do they get it?
- What writing utensils do students use, and what care do those utensils involve?

  - Who sharpens pencils?
  - What pens are okay, and what aren't?
  - How do we keep pens so that they last and don't burst open with ink?

- How do we access and sign into devices, and how should work be organized?
- Where can students work within the classroom?

The more that community members know, understand, and agree to the answers to these questions, the better the community will function as a whole.

CHARTS AND RESOURCES WITHIN THE ENVIRONMENT

Charts, tools, and resources are both instructional elements and environmental elements, and you'll want to make sure that your classroom offers students ways to build independence without overwhelming them. When students are involved in developing the resources within their classroom, there are several positive results. First, students understand the rationale and the purpose of a tool if they've helped choose or create it. Additionally, students feel more ownership of their learning when they've helped plan and design it (Fletcher, 2008).

At a recent workshop for new teachers, I emphasized the importance of unfilled spaces when they welcome students into their classrooms. We toured several classrooms, and everyone could feel the difference between classrooms with lots of materials already on the walls and classrooms with blank spaces waiting to be developed. "The blank spaces are less overwhelming," one teacher reflected. "And they are sending a message that we'll develop the room together," another teacher added.

Exactly.

These two new teachers hit on two important points. For one, it's important to remember that the beginning of the year feels stressful for many students, and too much stimulation may add to that stress. Think about the experience of walking into a loud and raucous environment with neon colors and flashing lights, as opposed to an environment with quiet music and neutral colors. You want your classroom to be a place of laughter and joy, but not a place that accosts the senses.

Minimalism is welcome as you begin the school year, and, as you teach, you'll develop your classroom along with the students. That co-creation will build and nurture the sense of community that will inspire students as writers and as people. Students will not only *understand* their environment, but they also will have ownership of it.

Notes

How Do I Engage and Communicate With Families/Caregivers?

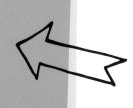

At the time I am writing this, we've completed a school year in which many students attended school from home, and caregivers played more active roles in their children's educational lives than ever. Before and after the pandemic of 2020, engagement and communication with families and caregivers about students' writing lives have the potential to accelerate learning and excitement. There are a few ways you can ensure that parents are partners in students' writing lives.

REACH OUT EARLY IN THE YEAR

Engagement and communication with families/caregivers can begin even before the school year with welcoming messages and questions about what's important to students. Caregivers have the power to provide insights and information that will help you when students struggle in the idea-generating stage. Depending on the family's circumstances, you can use digital or physical mediums to ask questions. Some questions you might ask caregivers include, but aren't limited to:

- What are some of your child's favorite activities to do alone? To do together?
- Who are some of the important people in your child's life?
- What are some of your child's favorite places?
- What does your child do when there is free time?

The answers to any of these questions become potential stories!

Caregivers can also provide insights as to their child's past experiences with writing. You can ask about favorite past writing pieces, least favorite pieces, as well as any sort of writing life a child has outside of school. It's easy to overlook list-making, family calendars, and thank-you notes as important writing moments.

Your belief set is foundational and important to share. If you have a curriculum night, offer an overview of the language, systems, and structures of your writing community, and invite caregivers to use the language and duplicate parallel structures in their home environment. Just as teachers set up systems and structures in classrooms, caregivers can set up workspaces for children within their homes. You might even provide a checklist of writing supplies for students to write at home, as well as extra copies of relevant classroom charts.

A possible checklist of writing supplies for student writers at home:

- ☐ Paper
    - ☐ Narrative writing paper
    - ☐ Information writing paper
    - ☐ Opinion for writing paper
    - ☐ Blank paper
- ☐ Writing utensils

☐ Computer or another electronic device
☐ Charts
☐ Checklists

You may decide to send a list of language terms, a checklist, or a series of newsletters. (Remember when I mentioned how hard it is for people to identify as writers? When you write family newsletters, you are a writer!) Whatever you decide on, it's important that caregivers know and understand the beliefs, languages, and structures of their child's writing life in school.

CONTINUE TO COMMUNICATE

As the year progresses, you can maintain communication and engagement. Letting families know when a unit is ending and what is upcoming helps them ask pertinent questions. For example, if you're in the middle of a narrative unit, it's great to provide caregivers with questions, prompts, and activities that could support writers.

Ideas to Support Narrative Writing at Home

1. Ask your child to tell you stories, and help them structure the stories into a beginning, middle, and end format. Your interest will inspire them to want to add the details that make it a story, and telling stories is an important precursor to writing stories.

2. Tell your child stories—ones from your childhood, ones from your days. Your child will love hearing about your life, and listening to stories will help develop an understanding of how to tell stories.

3. Notice and point out the stories that happen in your daily living, such as cleaning up a mess, misplacing and finding your glasses, or deciding on a TV show.

You can develop these sorts of prompts and lists, as well as letters of explanation, for any unit you are working on at school, and I have included some samples on the companion website (resources.corwin.com/answerselementarywriting). The more caregivers know and understand, the more they can help.

In addition to prompts, you can also create toolkits for writers to use when they are not in the classroom. These toolkits may take the form of small charts, checklists, letter boards, word lists, or highlighted texts. They should consist of resources writers know and can explain that help them write. When you and writers can explain the tools and how they help, then you can engage families and caretakers in using or duplicating such resources in their home environment.

SHARE STUDENT WRITING

Many caregivers want to see student writing, and sharing pieces is an important way to engage them. When you do share, it's important to explain the process and the growth of writers. Many adults expect final pieces to look perfect, yet that might not be the case. Consider crafting messages that explain the process and purpose of the writing instruction that's been happening leading up to the piece that heads home. For example:

> In this unit, we thought about how to teach others about a topic we knew a lot about. We tried to create sections that organized our information, and we worked hard to introduce our topics in ways that would interest readers. We also thought about the different ways we could teach readers through pictures, diagrams, or other text features. We worked on spelling and punctuation, as well, but those might not be perfect since we were trying to use new words that related to our topic.

You may also use sticky notes on student writing to communicate the part of the process or the specific trait or element of writing that was the focus for this particular piece of writing. This practice may help caregivers understand and appreciate the importance of process in the lives of writers.

What Resources Should I Have Available to Support Students' Independence?

PHYSICAL RESOURCES FOR STUDENTS TO ACCESS

As a special education teacher, I worked closely with a classroom teacher who prioritized and emphasized the importance of classroom charts. "Do they really use those charts?" a visitor asked us. Rather than answer ourselves, we had the visitor ask the students. "Definitely," one of the fifth-graders responded. "When I'm stuck and the teachers are busy, I can look at it and remember something that helps me."

Some of the resources I recommend creating and nurturing include:

- Classroom charts: It's worth knowing the different types of charts and ways to make them as user-friendly as possible.
- Mentor texts: Reading and writing are reciprocal processes, and the more that students read with an appreciation of craft, the stronger their reading skills become. Their writing skills also improve as they work to emulate how an admired writer does something in a text.
- Checklists: The more you can develop and inspire students to use checklists that detail what their writing texts should include, the more independently students will work. Student-friendly language and pictures/graphics are helpful for increasing the use of checklists.
- Partnerships: Most writers, regardless of age and experience, have critical friends. The more students know and understand how to use partners, asking questions and offering meaningful feedback, the more independence you will see in your classroom of writers.

A worthwhile activity to do with students in your classroom is to ask them to stand near something that helps them work independently. You can ask them to move from resource to resource, paying attention to where many students go and where few go. You can learn a lot by asking them what helps them learn and develop independence. These tools and resources build your writing community since they establish the importance and expectation of independence.

Agency and Identity

You'll read over and over about the importance of students co-creating charts with you. When students are part of making those charts, students share in the ownership, build their own agency within learning, and are more apt to use them!

Answers to Your Biggest Questions About Teaching Elementary Writing

DIGITAL RESOURCES FOR STUDENTS TO ACCESS

During the 2020–2021 school year, many resources that had only appeared in live classrooms were re-envisioned and re-created for a virtual platform. Teachers can provide tools for independence through many platforms. For example, if the students are used to Google Classroom, teachers can post digital representations of charts. They can even post those representations right on student writing, directing students to delete the picture when they are finished with the section. These pictures and charts serve as scaffolds that enable students to remember and practice skills they might not be able to without the visual reminder, but might not need after such intentional practice. These resources become part of the classroom community, and they can also be extended to families and caregivers.

Figure 1.9 Padlet is a tool for organizing and sharing resources.

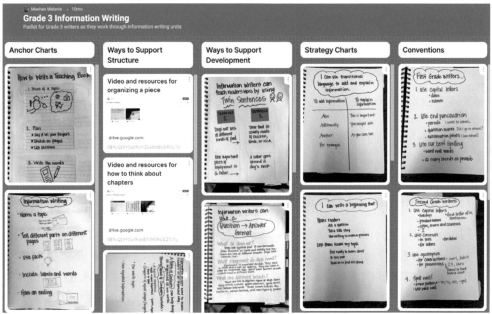

Great Resources

Padlet is another resource that allows teachers to share many types of resources for building independence. You can explore the Padlet for third-grade information writers through the QR code.

resources.corwin.com/
answerselementarywriting

To read a QR code, you must have a smartphone or tablet with a camera. We recommend that you download a QR code reader app that is made specifically for your phone or tablet brand.

What Resources Should I Have Available to Support Students' Independence?

33

COMMUNITY

How Do I Establish a Risk-Taking Environment That Feels Safe, Supportive, and Joyful?

My oldest daughter, Larkin, is a professional artist, and she has worked for several companies. She will tell you that she creates her best work when she has artistic freedom but also in environments where she feels authentically happy.

ESTABLISH AN ASSET-BASED APPROACH

An asset-based approach, stated simply, comes at instruction from the question of what students are able to do. Many times, teaching begins with what students need to learn. The difference is subtle but important because focusing on their assets has the potential to shift students' mindsets, inviting them into the learning process with a feeling of confidence rather than intimidation.

Let's look at how to evaluate a piece of writing by looking through an asset-based lens. The following narrative was written by a fifth-grade student at the beginning of a narrative writing unit. Let's think about all this writer is already doing.

The Beginning of a Grade 5 Narrative

It was only about 4:00 when my mom and dad brung me and my sibling to Six Flags FRIGHT FEST. I was only 8 and I was a scared little kid. I didn't like zombies, clowns or even ghosts. It took us an hour because the line was so long it was as long as the great wall of China. One hour later we finally and officially got into six flags with our passes. Once we got in there was a photographer that took a picture of us. The photographer left and started to laugh and there you know it "ahhhhhhhhhh" there was a tall creepy looking clown that was just smiling and that's when I thought what type of nightmares am I going to have tonight.

What this writer is doing:

- Setting up a setting
- Establishing the characters in the scene
- Providing some background information
- Using transitional language to show the passage of time
- Trying out some figurative language
- Setting a mood through the use of "ahhhhhhhhhh"

No doubt that there are teaching points to take on for this writer, as well. Paragraphing, sentence fluency, and the use of dialogue could all be taught to this writer. I might sit down next to him, provide feedback about what he's doing, and then ask what he's specifically working on. Depending on his response, I could address his stated goal or I could move into the reasons writers use paragraphs. However, leading with and noticing what the writer *can* do, as opposed to what the writer *can't* do, is an asset-based approach and leads to a more positive-thinking student and overall community.

As you work on an asset-based approach, you may find the consideration of these shifts to be helpful:

Instead of . . .	Try this . . .
How is it going?	May I join you? What are you working on?
What do I think the writer should learn?	What does the writer think they should learn?
What do I need to teach?	What do I need to celebrate?
What can I teach this writer?	What can I learn from this writer?

Students are perceptive, and writing is vulnerable work. Therefore, the more you can lean into the positives and strengths of writers, the more power you have to build a positive writing community.

LANGUAGE TWEAKS

The more you can train yourself to use statements that signify respect and expectation for students, the more likely you will see them rise to the occasion as writers. As you think about how you deliver messages to students, there are slight revisions you might make that have the potential for significant changes.

Some Statements That Signify an Asset-Based Approach	
Statement	**Rationale for the Asset-Based Approach Component**
What are you working on?	This question assumes that students are both working and that they are working on something. Both assumptions communicate the expectation of positive intent and mindset from students.
What are you proud of in this piece of writing?	Again, this question conveys the belief that the student has elements of writing to discuss and celebrate.
Let's think about next steps for you.	The suggestion of next steps indicates that there have already been steps taken.
You're not using paragraphs in your writing yet, but I think you're ready.	The use of the word *yet* often communicates the expectation that there's a possibility.

NORMALIZE NEXT STEPS/RISK-TAKING

In *Mindset,* Carol Dweck (2008) emphasizes the importance of a growth mindset. By studying the behavior of thousands of children, Dweck described growth mindset as the underlying belief that effort makes people stronger and leads to higher achievement. This finding is foundational in the creation of a writing community where the goal is not perfection but, instead, the focus is on answering questions like How can I make this better? and What have I learned from this piece? This is crucial for writing instruction that's focused on process over product!

Some key ways for developing this thought process include:

- Modeling your own writing process with an emphasis on work in progress and not completed/perfect work.
- Differentiating between "published" and "perfect." Published pieces can be reflective of what students are working on and do not need to be free of mistakes.
- Creating a shared understanding within the community of the writing process and the different entry points into it. There is not a formula for writing a piece and the flexibility may provide some students with more security to engage in the process. I go more into different entry points in Chapter 3.
- Celebrating progress and goal-setting.

Notes

How Do We Celebrate Progress as a Community?

When you are teaching writing with unit-based instruction, you are spending a planned amount of time in that unit, and there is a beginning and an ending to the focus on a type of writing. For example, you may teach students how to write an informational text over a 4–6 week stretch of the year. During that unit, it's important to have some planned days for celebration.

CREATE CELEBRATIONS *DURING* THE UNIT

There are some celebrations that can happen during the unit. If you've established anchor charts and you've encouraged the use of checklists, these celebrations might be about what writers have learned to do so far in the unit. For example, you might have a Checklist Celebration, where students go over the skills and descriptions on a checklist, indicating the elements they can show in their writing, the ones they're working on, and the ones they haven't started yet.

Keep in Mind

When students are filling out checklists, it's important to establish that their writing should be out and side by side with the checklist. If they are checking the yes-box, they should be able to point out exactly where their writing has evidence of that indicator.

Another mid-unit celebration involves asking students to share a favorite part of their current piece and inviting other students to provide feedback for the writer. The more specific students make their feedback, the better for the entire writing community.

Mid-Unit Celebrations	
Checklist Celebration	Students fill out checklists or portions of checklists reflecting on what they've learned and what some next steps could be.
Partial Share	Students read favorite parts of their work in progress, and others provide feedback.
Goal-Setting Celebrations	Students move from writing piece to writing piece on the hunt for goals they can work on themselves.

Goal-setting celebrations involve students reading each other's writing, but with the lens of what they can learn from that writer and try to emulate themselves as writers. This sort of celebration also builds a stronger writing community as students notice and note each other's strengths and potential for being a resource.

COMMIT TO CELEBRATIONS *AT THE END* OF A UNIT

The First Grade Tea was a major event in my daughters' lives because they all loved writing and received a lot of positive attention for their stories, but it was probably not a positive event for many families. End-of-unit celebrations don't need to involve families and cookies and punch bowls and tablecloths. In fact, all the hoopla changes the focus from the growth and process that happened throughout the unit to the product that's associated with the end. This is not a positive change for many writers in your classroom. Remember, you want to create a celebration that incorporates joy, pride, and excitement—and not stress, worry, and fear.

One of my favorite end-of-unit celebrations is a compliment celebration. Play some soft background music and invite students to move from desk to desk reading each other's writing and leaving complimentary feedback. (You'll find a downloadable Compliment Sheet on the online companion website, resources.corwin.com/answerselementarywriting.) Throughout the celebration, you can challenge students to read and leave different comments, using the classroom tools and resources to remind them of some of the elements they can be looking for.

Depending on the length of pieces and the size of the class, you can have students read their pieces out loud in a special author's chair, inviting community members to again offer compliments and positive feedback. If you are partnered with another older or younger classroom, invite that class to come in and listen to writing pieces in partnerships or as a whole group.

Perhaps more than anything else, when it comes to celebrations, focus on the growth and the processes that led to it. When this focus is clear, students have more clarity of what they are learning, teachers have more effective feedback, and transfer, the goal of instruction, is more likely to be happening.

 Agency and Identity

Padlet is an effective way to invite students to share their work. By using the "Shelf" option within the Padlet platform, each student can have their own column. They can display their work at the top of the column, and classmates can leave comments and compliments below. Since Google Docs allows students to make comments, this is another way to facilitate a digital compliment celebration.

Answers to Your Biggest Questions About Teaching Elementary Writing

How Do I Communicate the Importance, Power, and Joy That Writing Brings?

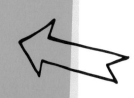

In his book, *Creating Innovators*, Tony Wagner (2012) shares his research that students who become innovators have passion, purpose, and play at the core of what they are studying. The more opportunities for all three, the more positive energy appears in a writing community.

COMMUNICATE THE IMPORTANCE AND POWER OF WRITING

Throughout history, writing has been a skill and a privilege, intentionally shared and withheld to maintain or limit power. Understanding the why of anything leads to greater buy-in, engagement, and success. Students should learn the importance of writing in their lives, and asking this question can be the start of a great inquiry. You can invite students to share their reasons for writing and its importance in their lives with inquiry questions such as:

- Why is it important to know how to write?
- Why is writing important in my life now, my life in the future, and in the lives of people around me?
- When and how has writing been important throughout history or during a particular historical event?

You want students who understand and appreciate the power of writing and don't just see it as an act of compliance. Writing is a way to entertain, to inform, and to persuade. It's a way to impact the world, as well as find meaning and deeper understandings in and about life.

INFUSE JOY AND PLAY INTO WRITING

On a lighter but just as important note, pay attention to the joy that is in your writing classroom. While joy happens through emotional experiences, it also happens through fun and play. Consider ways to bring humor into writing instruction because humor is a powerful way to infuse joy into the community. Reading aloud funny books and using them as mentor texts is one way to do this. Another way is to involve students in the analysis and creation of jokes. Many jokes involve plays on words or language structure, and they also offer great low-stakes practice for conventions and grammar.

Multimedia experiences also have a lot of potential for bringing humor into the classroom. Offer up a series of pictures and challenge students to write captions. These memes are likely to get everyone laughing and may also inspire fully developed stories.

Great Resources

• Cunningham, K. E. (2019). *Start with joy: Designing literacy learning for student happiness*. Stenhouse.

• Edwards, K. (2021, May 19). The serious business of laughter in the classroom. *We Are Teachers*. https://www.weareteachers.com/laughter-in-the-classroom

• Meehan, M., & Peterson, G. (2019, May 20). Bringing humor into writing workshops. *Two Writing Teachers*. https://twowritingteachers.org/2019/05/20/bringing-humor-into-writing-workshops

• Moore, B. (2021, March 18). Making space in writing workshop for kids to be funny. *Two Writing Teachers*. https://twowritingteachers.org/2021/03/18/making-space-for-kids-to-be-funny

Beyond humor, also consider ways to infuse play into the writing community. You can create games for developing and combining sentences, and these sorts of activities are not just playful; these activities develop flexibility and strengthen students' use and understanding of language. In addition to word-oriented games, many students love the challenge of creating or keeping a story going, secret sentence by secret sentence. Activities such as "pass the story" are low-stakes and low-pressure, and they strengthen students' ability to recognize and appreciate story structure.

Games to Play in Your Writing Community

• MadLibs: Students provide various parts of speech without seeing the whole of the story.

• Stretch a Sentence: Students change short sentences into longer sentences, a game that can be differentiated based on readiness and understanding.

• Add a Clause: Students change a sentence by adding a clause. To add to the challenge, you can ask them to add clauses in various parts of the original sentence.

• Combine a Sentence: Give students two or more sentences with the challenge to combine the sentence.

• Continue a Story: Students write the next sentence or event of a story and then pass it so that only their part of it shows.

End-of-Chapter Reflections

What might you try within the next week? The next month?

When you think back on your year of writing instruction, what do you want students to know and believe about themselves as writers?

What are three ways that you can work toward those beliefs?

How Do I Communicate the Importance, Power, and Joy That Writing Brings?

41

WHAT SHOULD STUDENTS KNOW AND BE ABLE TO DO AS WRITERS?

Not long ago, a colleague brought me a sample of writing by a child, Charlie, she'd been asked to tutor over the summer before he entered third grade. Admittedly, I had to read the writing two or three times to understand some of the words the child had approximated spelling. Additionally, the letter formation was off in some places, and some might have said it looked sloppy. However, once I read it out loud, my colleague and I smiled. The child's writing was full of insight, humor, and explanation of sophisticated ideas about a book and characters.

As you read this chapter, think about what constitutes effective writing and how you translate those concepts for students. The more *you* understand and have clarity around what is "good" writing, the more *students* will understand, as well.

Charlie's writing piece is representative of how difficult it is to distill and define good writing. There's a subjectivity that undermines consistent and reliable expectations and evaluation of writing. Furthermore, without a clear process and definable steps, it's even harder to determine mastery and understanding. This chapter focuses on the curriculum and expectations of proficient writing—and it takes on some of the nebulous questions of what makes for good writing and what should students learn next so that you feel more confident and competent in your instructional approach.

This chapter answers the following questions:

- [ ] **What types of writing are there, and how are they similar and different?**
- [ ] **What are the features of effective writing?**
- [ ] **How should I think about and guide students' writing processes?**
- [ ] **What is the difference between process and product, and why does it matter for student writing?**
- [ ] **What is the importance of volume for student writers, and how can I keep the energy and output high?**
- [ ] **How do grammar and conventions fold into writing and instruction?**
- [ ] **How do I plan a sequence for the year?**

You'll want to think about the curriculum, units, and lessons you teach students as you read this chapter, constantly evaluating how you can use the curriculum and the goals you have for student writers to foster high levels of learning and growth within your writing instruction.

What Types of Writing Are There, and How Are They Similar and Different?

Through a comprehensive search for studies evaluating instructional practices that improve student writing, Graham and colleagues (2012) provide several recommendations for writing instruction. The recommendation with the strongest evidence to support it involves teaching students to use the writing process and write for a variety of purposes. Students need to learn how to shift their communication styles depending on purpose and audience, skills that are complex but also intentional and motivating. The more students know and understand the genres of writing, the better they will be able to revise their pieces and address their audience.

THREE MAIN TYPES OF WRITING

As a writing teacher, you'll want to know the three main genres of writing that the Common Core (and most other state/local standards; see www.corestandards.org/ELA-Literacy/) address: narrative, information, and opinion. (See the following section in this chapter.) Poetry is sometimes its own entity but can be any one of the three genres as well. Even though writing genres overlap, it is helpful to categorize and understand them to structure units and logical teaching points.

You can teach the types of writing and the characteristics of each one explicitly, providing direct instruction (see Chapter 3) and plenty of examples through mentor texts that students read or that you read aloud. This knowledge helps them access instruction about the genre that will help them write better.

Type of Writing	Description or Definition	Examples
Narrative	Tells a story	Personal narrative, realistic fiction, graphic novels, fantasy or imaginative fiction, fairy tales
Information	Teaches the audience	Reports, feature articles, podcasts, informational essays
Opinion/Argument	Offers an opinion, claim, or argument	Opinion essays, editorials, TED Talks, literary essays
Poetry	Takes many forms, but written in lines or stanzas and incorporates a variety of figurative language to convey meaning and create images	Free verse, rhymed poems, narrative poems, haikus, sonnets, and many others

Keep in mind, there is crossover among genres. Some examples might include:

- Strong opinion writing frequently uses facts and information as evidence to provide rationale and support for the opinion.

- The use of an anecdote, a narrative technique, also may strengthen opinion writing.
- Within an information piece, there may also be evidence of the writer's opinion. For example, an informational report on colonial America may include an opinion essay about whether it was better to be a colonial boy or girl. An informational piece about dogs may include an opinion section on why big dogs are better than small dogs.
- Narrative techniques may also show up in the other genres. Stories engage audiences and therefore belong in many reports and essays. The classroom chart shown in Figure 2.1 shows ways to include story elements in informational texts.

Including these sorts of features develops students' understanding and differentiation between different types of writing, which you want to develop.

Keep in Mind

No matter what genre you are focused on at a specific time over the course of the year, you want students to be able to access previously taught material. Narrative writing has power within information and opinion writing! Consider teaching an explicit lesson about how to include narrative techniques within information and opinion writing, as shown in Figure 2.1 of a co-created chart.

Figure 2.1 There are several ways for students to add narrative writing into informational texts.

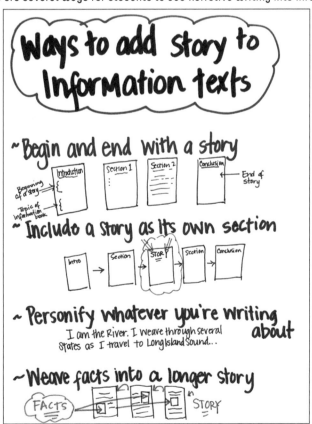

THE POWER OF POETRY

Poetry does not show up in the Common Core State Standards or many state standards as its own genre, but there are many ways to reinforce language and traits of writing through it. Poetry has the power to tell a story, and it can also inform or present an opinion. Additionally, poetry is a meaningful way to address language standards. You can notice, note, and challenge students to emulate decisions around punctuation through poetry. Through a poetry platform, you can also emphasize figurative language, sentence structure, and repetition as craft moves writers can use regardless of genre to increase voice and fluency in their writing.

Notes

What Are the Features of Effective Writing?

One of the challenges with identifying the features of effective writing is that there are so many different genres. How can you compare narrative writing to information writing? And what about poetry? Can you relate and compare poetry to opinion writing? While each genre has its own expectations, there are commonalities between all types of writing, and the more you can be on the lookout for the common threads, the more comfortable you will be identifying and developing strong writing. Traits of writing and categories of writing, both described in this section, can be effective lenses for thinking about, talking about, and teaching aspects of effective writing.

More than anything else, effective writing boils down to **the precision of language to express thoughts clearly**. Is the writer able to express themselves with clarity for readers to understand and follow? Given a bank of knowledge, a belief, or a story, is a writer able to express and share their thoughts? When readers understand the intentions of writers, writers are doing their jobs!

TRAITS OF WRITING

It's helpful to think of writing traits when analyzing the quality of student writing. Ruth Culham (2003) identifies six specific traits as features of effective writing— ideas, word choice, sentence fluency, voice, organization, and conventions, with one additional consideration of the overall presentation. You can use these traits both in assessing writing to help students reach for the next level, and you can teach these traits to children as they draft and revise.

As I think about the trait of **ideas**, I think about whether a writer is able to identify writing topics, recognizing moments that can become stories, topics of expertise, and beliefs or opinions that are explainable. The more students can find story-worthy moments in their lives, as well as tap into their own funds of knowledge, curiosity, and opinions, the more invested they will become in their own writing. The introduction emphasizes the importance of choice for writers, but students have to be able to or learn how to find their writing topics.

Writers should also be aware of their **word choice** and pay attention to the vocabulary they are using, the audience they are addressing with it, the repetition of words, and the nuances of language. This aspect of writing is complex, and it's complicated to pinpoint precise ways to teach word choice and vocabulary. For example, many teachers lean into lessons about the various ways to change the word *said*. However, in books, authors use that word over and over because often it's the clearest, most direct word and keeps the rhythm of the dialogue in place. The more you can pay attention to nuances of language in what you read, trying to name what and why the language impacted you, the better you will become at teaching word choice, vocabulary, and language nuances to students, important elements for developing voice in student writing.

CURRICULUM

CURRICULUM

There is a progression that happens within communication when it comes to **sentence fluency** as writers learn how to use and manipulate language, varying sentence structure, complexity, and phrasing. Another way that writer's voice comes through is via the complexity and variation of sentence structure, vocabulary choices, repetition, and other craft moves.

Voice is perhaps the most difficult trait to teach explicitly, as well as identify systematically. Voice involves more than the evaluation of whether a student's writing sounds like that student. It has more to do with the emotion that a writer is able to create in a piece of writing, and writers create emotion through a variety of craft moves. Language, sentence variety, grammatical decisions, and vocabulary all offer opportunities for writers to create voice. The more you can notice emotion in mentor texts (see Chapter 3), the more you can consider with students how the writer created that emotion, and the more you will begin to see voice in student writing.

Strong writing has a clarity of purpose, which I think of as focus or **organization**. If a writer is telling a story, do you know what the story is about? If you do, then chances are the writer did also, and the more students understand what their story is about—really, really about—then the better they are able to add relevant details and expand important parts. Information writing should have an organizational structure that helps both the writer create and the reader understand. Many information pieces lose their focus because the writer doesn't have enough information to sustain a section, not because the writer doesn't understand organization. Clarity of purpose is much easier to teach when a writer has plenty to say!

The trait of **conventions**, combined with the overall concept of **presentation**, frequently leads to wonderings about "Is this good writing?" as was the case for Charlie in the chapter-opening vignette. Like the other traits, there is a progression that should happen during the development of writers when it comes to conventions and spelling. It's worth spending the time learning what is expected in your own teaching community based on a scope and sequence or a set of standards when it comes to conventions. Asking students to be accountable for all punctuation, capitalization, and spelling runs the risk of shutting off their creativity and bravery as new writers, a balance that you have to be careful of! (Remember that sentence fluency trait? Sometimes it requires bending the rules of conventions.)

Finally, the **presentation** trait should be evaluated based on what you've communicated to students about the goals and criteria for the particular piece. In other words, if this is a rough draft, there can be strike-throughs, but if it's a final, polished piece of writing for an envisioned audience, then neatness and presentation should matter.

Trait	Questions to Consider Can the Writer . . . ?
Ideas	• Identify writing topics • Recognize moments that can become stories • Identify topics of expertise • Explain beliefs and opinions

Trait	Questions to Consider Can the Writer . . . ?
Word Choice	• Attend to the words they are choosing • Appreciate and explain nuances of language • Select words and vocabulary for an envisioned and specific audience
Fluency	• Vary sentence structure to interest and engage audience • Use structures of language, such as repetition • Combine sentences or insert additional information into them
Voice	• Combine sentence structure, word choice, and fluency to create an intentional mood
Organization	• Provide a clarity of purpose • Group ideas with an awareness of audience • Establish a sequence or structure
Conventions	• Use capital letters intentionally and correctly • Guide readers with intentional punctuation • Use accurate spelling given the writer's developmental level
Overall Presentation	• Exhibit or present message on paper • Balance white space with print and text • Incorporate graphics, font, and text features • Demonstrate neatness and overall appearance

CURRICULUM

THREE CATEGORIES TO USE AS YOU CONSIDER EFFECTIVE WRITING

Another way to consider effective writing is to think about categories instead of traits. Calkins and colleagues (2014) and the Common Core rubrics divide the qualities of effective writing into three categories: structure, development, and conventions. Regardless of genre, effective writing has a structure that consists of a beginning, middle, and end. When writers attend to structure, their writing maintains the focus and precision required to communicate with clarity. Also regardless of genre, good writing has development. In narrative writing, that development involves how the writer uses relevant dialogue, description, action, and inner thinking, while in other genres, writers blend facts and evidence with explanation and connections. All these elements combine with the intentional use of conventions and grammar to make for effective written communication.

These categories could be part of the common language described in Chapter 1, which helps establish a community. As you develop your understanding of structure, development, and conventions, you can begin to think of how they relate to the various genres.

Category	Genre	Features
Structure	Narrative	A clear beginning, middle, and end
	Information	An introduction, clear sections of categorized information, and a conclusion
	Opinion	An introduction that includes a claim, paragraphs that relay reasons and explanations, and a conclusion
Development	Narrative	The blending of dialogue, description, action, and inner thinking
	Information	The use and explanation of facts and examples, blending of independent thinking and analysis, use of text features
	Opinion	The incorporation and explanation of evidence
Conventions	Narrative, information, and opinion	The intentional use of capitalization and punctuation Attention to spelling The intentional use of tenses, pronouns, and verb consistency*

*I have purposely and intentionally avoided the term "correct" because different dialects and communities have different interpretations of correct, and there is not a universal correct form of usage. What is correct in one community may not be correct in another.

Keep in Mind

If you spend too much energy on students' correct use of conventions, spelling, and grammar, you may not spend enough time teaching into and celebrating students' abilities to generate, plan, and draft engaging pieces. Although conventions and spelling matter, writing is complex and involves the integration of many cognitive processes!

Agency and Identity

The use of capital letters frequently lags behind students' knowledge of *when they should* use them. Think about it as a habit, and remind students, sometimes several times during an independent writing session, to pay attention and check their last sentence for capital letters. Your reminders may lead to students paying attention *on their own* to capital letters as part of their process.

Great Resources

- Calkins, L., Hohne, K. B., & Robb, A. K. (2014). *Writing pathways: Performance assessments and learning progressions, grades K–8.* Heinemann.

- Culham, R. (2014). *The writing thief: Using mentor texts to teach the craft of writing.* International Reading Association.

- Culham, R. (2018). *Teach writing well: How to assess writing, invigorate instruction, and rethink revision.* Stenhouse.

- Heard, G. (2013). *Finding the heart of nonfiction.* Heinemann.

CURRICULUM

How Should I Think About and Guide Students' Writing Processes?

In addition to the traits and expectations of whatever genre they are working on, students should know and understand the parts of the writing process. The writing process has definite stages—generating ideas, planning, drafting, revising, and editing—but these stages are rarely linear, and the way writers move through each stage is a matter of personal style. For instance, when Kelsey Sorum and I co-wrote *The Responsive Writing Teacher* (2021), we realized that Kelsey's writing process had a much longer stage of planning. I am less of a planner and more of a reviser; to move a piece forward, Kelsey needs outlines, while I need words on a page. Figures 2.2 and 2.3 show the differences in our processes.

Figures 2.2 and Figure 2.3 Kelsey and Melanie share their own writing processes.

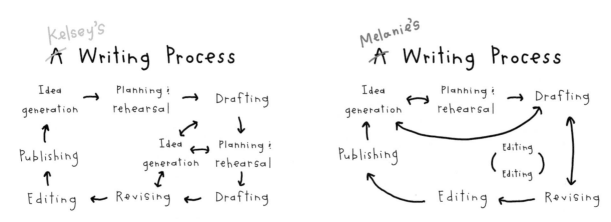

Source: Meehan & Sorum (2021).

TEACH STUDENTS ABOUT THE WRITING PROCESS AND ITS VARIATIONS

The parts of a writing process should make up part of the writing community's language (see Chapter 1), and students should have a solid understanding of what they are.

- **Generating**: Generating is the process of coming up with ideas for writing. Most writers have topics or ideas that they return to over and over, regardless of genre.
- **Planning**: Planning is how writers set up a system for knowing what they will write and how their piece will go. Not all writers plan the same way, and not all systems work for all writers. The more students understand the role of planning in their own writing lives, the more effectively they will work through this part of the writing process.
- **Drafting**: Drafting involves getting the words out on paper or digitally. It's important for writers to know that drafting does not imply completion, and it

also does not exclude or preclude revising and planning. Parts of the writing process are recursive and overlapping.

- **Revising**: Revising involves making changes with the goal of improvement. Students should learn that revising happens across the stages of the writing process.
- **Editing**: Editing involves the use of capitalization, punctuation, and spelling. Editing is NOT a separate stage in the writing process. It's important to encourage writers to use punctuation as they draft. Of course, there will be reviews and rereads that correct editorial mistakes, but students should not consider this to be a separate step.
- **Publishing**: The more that students envision an audience as they write, the more authentically they will see themselves as writers. Establishing the purpose and audience for writers as they are working their way through a writing piece paves their way toward meaningfully sharing their writing, whether it's for classmates, a loved one, or a public platform. Students will invest more deeply in their own writing pieces if they know their authentic purpose, which is synonymous with publication.

Students should learn that there's a circular and recursive process they can think of as an anchor for comparison: writers generate ideas, plan, draft, revise, revise plans, edit, draft, and revise again. Teachers can guide students to understand their own process and progression, creating an awareness and appreciation of some students' need to plan extensively before drafting, as opposed to other students' time spent revising an initial draft. There is not a specific amount of time required for any one step, and you will find variation between students. You may even find variation within the *same* student's process for different pieces of writing.

Figure 2.4 Regan's chart communicates her tendency to spend most of her writing time drafting.

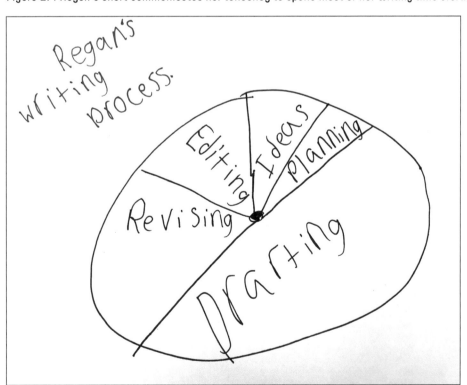

Figure 2.5 Jonah's chart reflects his challenge to come up with ideas, as well as his commitment to edit as he drafts.

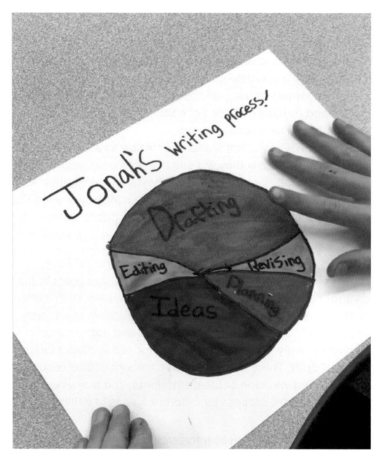

PROVIDE OPPORTUNITIES FOR STUDENTS TO ENTER THE PROCESS AT DIFFERENT POINTS

As you and students learn about each other's writing processes, you might recognize challenges and teaching opportunities because of the observations and understandings. For example, a student may struggle to think of an idea or topic but be able to plan and draft once a topic is available. In that case, it could be helpful to spend time reflecting, setting goals around, and teaching that student various strategies for finding writing topics. Additionally, that writer should appreciate and celebrate the skills that exist in the other parts of the writing process. Competence grows from confidence, and it's often more successful to teach from places of strengths and assets. Some students may experience more growth and success if they can enter the writing process at different points. The important thing is to recognize this and provide opportunities for practice so that students become able to navigate their own writing process from start to finish.

TEACH STUDENTS TO COLLABORATE DIFFERENTLY BASED ON WHERE THEY ARE IN THE PROCESS

The following chart shows some of the questions that students can lean into depending on the stage they or their partner is working on.

Stage	Questions to Ask or Pose
Generating	• What are times when you've had strong emotions or reactions? • What are some topics you love or know a lot about? • Who is someone you care about? • What would you like to change?
Planning	• What is your beginning, middle, and end? • What sections do you envision? • What are your reasons for thinking this?
Drafting	• How are you bringing your story to life? • What questions do you think your reader will have? • How can you explain your reason even better?

As you can see from the chart above, the deeper the understanding of the stage and the expectations, the more pertinent the questions and ensuing conversations can be.

Agency and Identity

The more you can engage students in becoming effective partners and collaborators, the more ownership they have over both their own learning and their classmates' learning. This ownership creates greater agency, and it also empowers you, the teacher, to reach and teach more students!

Keep in Mind

Do not think of editing as a separate step in the writing process. Instead, think of editing, especially when it comes to skills students have learned, as part of the drafting process.

How Should I Think About and Guide Students' Writing Processes?

55

What Is the Difference Between Process and Product, and Why Does It Matter for Student Writing?

In a reflective conversation, a relatively new writing teacher, Erin, commented that students wrote much stronger pieces as process pieces than as product pieces. Her comment led to some important insights about when and how students internalize new skills, and it's a complex distinction. "That's actually a really complicated question," I said to Erin. "Are you ready to think hard?"

Let's consider some of the differences between process, product, published, and polished.

Terms to Know

Process Piece: a piece of writing that a student works on over time, receiving input and suggestions throughout the process.

On-Demand Piece: a piece of writing that a student writes over the course of one to two writing periods that is reflective of what they know and are able to do as a writer.

LENGTH OF TIME

Throughout a six-week writing unit, most of the students in Erin's classroom had written one or two writing pieces, and she had conferred regularly with them, offering tips and providing direction for them to improve their stories. We referred to these pieces as the process pieces. At the end of the unit, Erin gave the students two days to write their best piece from start to finish. While they could use any resource in the room for reference or reminders, students were to create and write those pieces independently. These pieces were their on-demand pieces.

In primary classrooms, students may write several process pieces—sometimes even one a day—whereas as students progress through the grades, their pieces may take longer, given the increasing complexity of their work.

It's important to think of both process pieces and on-demand pieces as student products since, in both instances, students are creating something. However, process is *how* a student completes a piece, and product is *what* they create. Their process should involve learning, and their product should reflect what they've learned.

When we started the conversation, Erin was thinking of the pieces students wrote over the course of several days, with substantial teacher input as process pieces. She was thinking of pieces that students wrote over two writing sessions as product pieces. I coached her to think about both types of pieces as student-created products—just different types of products. The discrepancy between the two products suggested that she might have been teaching too much throughout the process. It's important to keep in mind that what you are teaching through a process piece should be within the possibility of internalization and transfer to an on-demand piece of writing. If a piece of process writing is too teacher-directed and the product is much more complex than the student can write when left to their own devices, then it's less likely for transfer to happen, which is the hallmark of authentic learning.

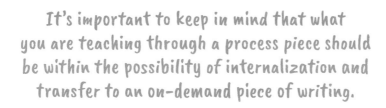

> It's important to keep in mind that what you are teaching through a process piece should be within the possibility of internalization and transfer to an on-demand piece of writing.

Throughout a writing unit, students should be engaged in a *process* that leads to a *product*, but they should be able to duplicate those processes with confidence and skill when asked to write an independent piece. It helped Erin to talk about the differences between process pieces, polished pieces, and products.

Terms to Know

Published Piece: the piece of writing that is shared within an established writing community. That community may vary, and the variation could change the expectations and the explanations of the work involved with the piece.

Polished Piece: the piece of writing that is mostly error-free, usually because a teacher or another adult has edited it, not necessarily with the understanding and collaboration of the student. (Truth: Even professional writers don't achieve perfection in their pieces, so I don't recommend aiming for perfection with students! I owe a debt of gratitude to one of the reviewers for suggesting *polished* instead of *perfect* pieces.)

Keep in Mind

Depending on the age of the students, process pieces may take several days. Younger students will take fewer days to create their products because their pieces are generally shorter and less complex than older writers. For all ages, process writing involves teaching and coaching and may reflect several teacher-directed revisions.

PURPOSE OF THE PIECE

Chapter 4 addresses assessment, and process writing falls within the umbrella of formative assessment because it should show teachers what students have learned, guiding teachers to make instructional decisions. On-demand writing can serve as either formative or summative, depending on how you use it. If you are using it to adjust instruction, then consider it as formative assessment. If you are evaluating students' transfer or learning and you will be moving on, then it serves as a summative assessment. It helped this teacher to realize that not every piece has to be polished, exhibiting every taught skill; some pieces are for practicing and isolating skills without the overwhelmingness of everything.

A product does not need to be perfect. It also does not need to demonstrate mastery of the skills a student might be working on at the time. An early writing piece may show evidence of organization, while a next piece may show evidence of both organization and word choice. Sometimes it helps to consider the pieces a student writes throughout a writing unit as a body of evidence to see the growth of the writer. To clarify what students are working on during any given piece, it helps to ask them regularly:

- What are you working on as a writer?
- What is a goal that you have for this piece of writing?

If you find that you are giving more suggestions and directives than the student is able to internalize and verbalize as self-assumed goals, then you may be putting too much emphasis on the product and not on the process of the student becoming a better writer.

Keep in Mind

Any corrections you make on a piece of student writing should be transferable by the student on to a future piece of writing. If a piece of writing is too full of teacher corrections, then the student learning may well be that they can't write successfully without a lot of coaching and corrections.

What Is the Importance of Volume for Student Writers, and How Can I Keep the Energy and Output High?

"I want to write a novel," Jenna, a fifth-grader, announced to me. A strong writer, she had developed her characters, envisioned a manageable plot, and established an outline. Over the next few weeks, I coached her as she drafted her way through several chapters. Unlike her peers, she was not bound by my "small-moment" story or a maximum of two pages or five scenes.

While there are expectations for production, these expectations are confounded by the issue that not all writing is high-quality writing. There are plenty of times when I've seen a student write reams of words that make little or no sense, while a peer writes a few lines that deliver a strong and clear message. Let's think about a child sitting down to play the piano. That child may sit and bang on the notes without any intention for melody or rhythm, and the production of notes could be the same or greater than the child who is working on mastering a song or a set of scales. One child is banging out notes, while the other child is engaged in intentional practice. The child banging on the piano is similar to the writer who uses ten *very*s in a row to express the magnitude of their anger. (*I was very, very, very, very, very ANGRY!!!!!!!!!*)

You can't know what a student is able to do if you don't have words to read, and a student can't practice new skills without opportunities to write more. And it's important to communicate the expectation that writing volume is created through intentional practice.

Sometimes it may seem counterintuitive, but stronger writers may be writing fewer pieces because, like Jenna, stronger writers can envision and wrangle a longer and more complex series of events without losing sight of the plotline or overall focus. These writers have internalized the structure of beginning, middle, and end, regardless of genre, and they can synthesize and integrate development strategies without losing the structural integrity of their piece. Less practiced writers, on the other hand, benefit from the routine of planning and drafting a piece with a focus and organization. This structure provides the gateway for the practice of relevant and intentional development and purposeful conventions.

"How many pieces should students write over the course of the unit?" teachers ask me frequently. While I don't purposely dodge my response to this question, the answer is complicated. Depending on the age of students and the type of writing, there is a range in the number of expected pieces. Some pieces may be important for mastery of some skills, while subsequent pieces may provide practice points for other skills. If students have higher skill levels and stamina, are invested in the revision process, and are writing longer, more elaborated stories, they may write two to three stories over the course of the unit. Writers who are developing skills and stamina will benefit more from writing several shorter stories that may not be fully developed but approximate clearer and clearer structure. Each piece may provide opportunities to practice specific skills and increase repertoire of knowledge and skills.

Terms to Know

Small-Moment Story: a story that takes place over a short period of time. Usually, small-moment stories are easier for writers to envision and develop since it's easier to establish the beginning, middle, and end, as well as the relevant and corresponding details.

Sometimes, the fewer expected pieces in a given writing unit, the greater the expectation is for the final product. When this happens, there is the potential for the focus to shift from the process to the product. This shift can decelerate learning. As you contemplate volume and the number of pieces, it helps to keep the focus on what students are learning and how they are growing as writers.

Agency and Identity

Don't be afraid to move writers on to a next piece of writing before they show mastery over a specific skill. Remember, you want to create opportunities for intentional practice and volume. Sometimes a new piece of writing will generate much more energy than any instructional strategy you can offer, and it will reveal the internalization and transfer of new skills—or the need for some reteaching.

Keep in Mind

Just as readers might occasionally "abandon" a book, writers might also abandon a writing piece. If this becomes a routine, then address it, but occasionally, allow the abandonment of a writing piece. You might ask a student: What did you learn about yourself as a writer from attempting this piece?

Notes

How Do Grammar and Conventions Fold Into Writing and Instruction?

Grammar and conventions are one of the first traits of writing that new teachers and caregivers want to address in student writing. Again, within a student's writing process, grammar and conventions may be considered as a separate step. However, students are more likely to internalize and transfer skills if they use what they know about language and punctuation as they draft. Explicit lessons may occur during an instructional block that targets skills such as capital letter usage, end punctuation, the use of commas, sentence variety, or inclusion of information through phrases. All these lessons build awareness of language and conventions, and awareness leads to intentional practice, approximation, and mastery.

BUILD AWARENESS OF GRAMMAR ACROSS LITERARY EXPERIENCES

The more you can build awareness of grammar and also create playful experiences around concepts that involve grammar, the more students will think about grammar and use it intentionally in their own writing. Here are a couple of ideas to use within your literacy instruction:

Notice and note the impact of powerful language usage in mentor texts and demonstration pieces. When you read with the lens of admiring sentence variety, you're likely to find it! Once you find it, have conversations about its impact. These conversations are likely to lead to students trying out these skills.

Invite students to play with language and conventions: Challenge students to combine sentences, which will develop their language skills. You might offer two related simple sentences and ask students to combine the ideas into one sentence with as many possibilities as possible, as in the example below:

The dog barked. The cat ran away.

- Because the dog barked, the cat ran away.
- When the dog barked, the cat ran away.
- The dog barked, and the cat ran away.
- If the dog barks, the cat runs away.
- The dog barked, so the cat ran away.
- The cat ran away when the dog barked.

Challenge students to lengthen a sentence. Most students are able to create a three- or five-word sentence: *I ran quickly* or *I ran to the house*. From there, how about a ten-word sentence or a twenty-word sentence?

- I ran quickly to the white house on the corner.
- I ran quickly to the white house on the corner, and then I walked the rest of the way home.

Terms to Know

Grammar: the intentional use of language to create impact and meaning.

Conventions: spelling and punctuation that help make writing readable and understandable.

CURRICULUM

How Do Grammar and Conventions Fold Into Writing and Instruction?

61

The more students notice grammatical craft moves and play with words and ways to combine them, the more fluency will show up in their writing.

PROVIDE INTENTIONAL PRACTICE FOR GRAMMAR CONCEPTS

Learning conventions requires repeated and intentional practice to shift from editing skills in isolation to mastery within composing and drafting. A scope and sequence of language use should include specific skills for specific grades. For example, in second grade, writers should use quotation marks around dialogue, while in third grade, they should use an end punctuation mark within those quotation marks. Knowing the scope and sequences empowers teachers to expect skills to show up in student writing and hold students accountable for intentional practice. With established expectations about the use of conventions, students have more opportunities for intentional practice that leads to mastery of punctuation, capitalization, and learned spelling rules.

Equity and Access

Display classroom and individual charts of conventions you expect to show up in student writing. These charts provide access when students are ready to take on a task or a skill, and they provide visual aids so students start to internalize and transfer new information.

Keep in Mind

Verbal rehearsal is a strategy that helps students remember information. Offer opportunities for verbal rehearsal where students are verbally stating the punctuation they would include. You may find that verbalizing the punctuation ahead of time helps students remember to include it in their writing.

How Do I Plan a Sequence for the Year?

THINK ABOUT THE UNITS YOU WILL TEACH THROUGHOUT THE YEAR

Many districts have a scope and sequence for writing instruction. If you do not have that, then think about creating a calendar with clear units of study that last four to six weeks, depending on the unit and the available instructional time.

If it's easier to think in terms of instructional minutes, then think of units consisting of 20 to 25 sessions of 45–60 minutes. You will want to have at least one unit for each of the three main genres: narrative, information, and opinion.

Additional units may include:

- Another round of any of the above three genres
- A launch unit that focuses on identity, past learning, structures, and systems of a writing class
- A poetry unit that emphasizes figurative language, word choice, and sentence structures
- Multimodal writing unit that offers an exploration of audio, video, and visual ways of communicating stories, information, or messages

Terms to Know

Scope and Sequence: what is covered throughout the lesson plans of a particular curriculum. The **scope** is the topics and areas of development within a curriculum, and the **sequence** is the order in which those skills are taught.

CREATE EXTRA WRITING UNITS AS NEEDED FOR STUDENTS TO PRACTICE SKILLS

As you consider the time you have for teaching students, you'll want to think in terms of units. At the end of those units, you have your chance to assess, reflect, and evaluate what students have learned and what may need some reteaching. The chart below offers suggestions for additional units within the categories of narrative, information, and opinion writing.

Additional Units That Address Genre-Based Skills		
Narrative	**Information**	**Opinion**
• Realistic fiction • Imaginative fiction • Graphic novels • Fantasy • Series	• Science reports • Biographies • Feature articles • News reports	• Letter writing • Editorials • Advertisements • Reviews: books, shows, restaurants, shops

Keep in Mind

Some students need extra practice to meet the goals of the curriculum. Pay attention to the genre students are striving to master the most. That genre would be a good one to return to. Pay attention as well to the high-energy genres and units because those are good to include at challenging instructional times like holidays and the end of the year.

INTEGRATE WRITING SKILLS INTO OTHER CONTENT AREAS

Knowing the genres of writing is important when considering opportunities to practice writing throughout the year. Maybe students need more practice writing narrative pieces, but they may benefit more from an integrated information or opinion piece. Think first about the various components of the content being studied, and within those sections, offer choices of writing pieces that feel authentic to that content. The following chart shows some examples.

Content Unit	Potential Narrative Topics	Potential Information Topics	Potential Opinion Topics
American Colonies	The time I learned to sew a hem on a dress	The various activities of children in early America	Explain whether it was better to be a girl or a boy during early America
Weather	The time a tree fell across the driveway in a hurricane	The different types of storms	Which storm is the most dangerous?
Living Things/ Animals	The time I saved a baby bird	Key characteristics of living things	What is the strongest or most dangerous animal?
Community	The time I went to a community event	Important parts of my community	Why is community important to people?
U.S. Geography	The time I visited a different state	Key parts of the geography of a specific state or region	Would you rather live near the ocean or near the mountains?

When you provide these writing opportunities for students, you'll want to remind them of the grade-level expectations. With those expectations in mind, students or teachers can make decisions about the type of writing they will use to express content and the expectations the content has.

In addition to providing students with independent writing opportunities through content, you can integrate writing into daily reflections, summaries of learning, and explanations of lessons through both shared writing experiences, interactive writing experiences, and other independent writing. Through any of these, you can emphasize and reinforce developing skills. (See Chapter 3 for a more in-depth discussion of these instructional strategies.)

End-of-Chapter Reflections

What might you try within the next week? The next month?

As you consider the students in your classroom, what are you prioritizing that they know and are able to do as writers?

What are three ways that you can work toward those goals?

chapter THREE

WHAT ARE KEY INSTRUCTIONAL PRACTICES TO KNOW AND USE?

While the focus of Chapter 2 is on curriculum—the *what* of teaching—this chapter delves into instruction, or the *how* of teaching. Teachers are constantly designing learning experiences for students, using strategies that promote student learning of the curriculum.

This chapter answers the following questions:

☐ **What is the principle of the zone of proximal development, and how does it relate to writing instruction?**

☐ **What are the different choices and models I have for instruction?**

☐ **How should I balance whole group instruction with small group and individualized instruction?**

☐ **What are the roles of both teacher and students within writing instruction?**

☐ **What resources do I need for high-impact instruction, and how do I introduce them?**

☐ **How do I balance approximation and intentional practice that leads to learning and mastery?**

☐ **What are some strategies I can use to provide entry points and to inspire additional practice when students need it?**

☐ **How do I balance scaffolding student learning with building foundational skills and understandings?**

This chapter focuses on instruction and how to engage students daily through various instructional models and effective record-keeping. As you read this chapter, think about the organization, structure, and management of your writing classroom. It addresses broad, overarching, instructional topics that carry out across the year.

What Is the Principle of the Zone of Proximal Development, and How Does It Relate to Writing Instruction?

During a professional development session, I asked a group of adults to stand up and touch their knees. Everyone did it. I asked them to touch their ankles. Almost everyone could touch their ankles, and even those who couldn't quite reach gave it a try. When I asked them to touch their toes without straightening their knees, there was more frustration in the room and even a few groans. People still laughed when I asked them to place their palms on the floor without bending their knees, but very few people even tried. A couple actually sat back in their chairs.

"That's the zone of proximal development in action," I said. "You'll get bored at a task that's too easy, you'll try at one that's a little hard, and you'll give up when you feel like you have no chance."

There were a lot of nods in the room when I suggested that figuratively, we do a lot of asking students to place their palms on the floor.

Lev Vygotsky (1978) introduced the zone of proximal development (ZPD) to the world of educators. The graphic shows the relationship of what people are able to do on their own, with a little scaffolding or assistance, and with heavy guidance. Tasks that are too simple may bore learners and do not lead to new learning. Tasks that are too difficult lead to frustration, and learners may understandably opt to give up. When learners face tasks that challenge them without overwhelming them, high learning rates take place.

Figure 3.1 The zone of proximal development emphasizes the relationship of what people are able to do on their own, with a little scaffolding or assistance, and with heavy guidance.

Source: Meehan & Sorum (2021).

Agency and Identity

If teachers are providing constant direction and guidance, then students are not growing as learners; instead, they are learning to wait for the next directive, which hinders their development of their academic potential. The more you consider the ZPD as you work with students, the more students will take on risks and gain independence, building agency and becoming more effective writers.

Writing involves the integration of many developing skills and cognitive processes. It involves memory, innovation, and information integration. Additionally, it involves the fine motor skills of pen or pencil to paper, as well as spelling, and the use of developing conventions. Therefore, it's important to constantly balance the introduction of new skills with the comfort of using developing ones and leaning into mastered skills to support new skill development.

When you look at the ZPD graphic, you can envision the band of learning as flexible. For some students, it's wider than for others because they have a greater tolerance for frustration. Additionally, for individual learners, that band may vary given the task and their history with it. Regardless, learners experience a physical high from brain chemicals when they accomplish something within their optimal band of learning (Hammond, 2014).

Confidence builds competence builds confidence in a recursive relationship, and the more opportunities you can offer students to experience the surge of success, the more effective your instruction will be on learning. In contrast, failure, even if it's perceived, can lead to stressful situations for students. Stressful situations trigger the release of cortisol, a stress hormone, which imparts the ability to learn (Cozolino, 2013). The combined message of this research underscores the importance of finding and teaching toward a learning sweet spot: a place where students feel curiosity, possibility, and power along their learning pathway.

Figure 3.2 Curiosity leads to competence and confidence in a recursive cycle.

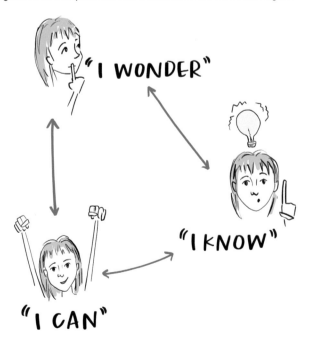

Keep in Mind

Competence connects directly with confidence, so it's imperative to know and understand how and why students do and don't feel confident about their writing.

Most packaged or purchased curriculum is based on a set of standards, and the developers create a series of lessons that address them. However, those lessons do not take into account the students in front of you and their readiness for the lessons. If the lessons are beyond students' ZPDs, you may have students shutting down and feeling frustrated. That sort of disengagement will not result in learning and growth. Therefore, there are times when you will need to understand the goals of the curriculum as well as the ways to navigate toward those goals along pathways that are accessible to students.

Even though writing can feel vulnerable to many students, writing has pathways with points of entry and progressions that lead to more success. The more you learn about writing instruction and its process, the more you will realize the recursiveness of the process, and it's that recursiveness that provides flexible entry points for students. Furthermore, drafting is only a component of writing, and other components, especially revision, lead to stronger and stronger pieces, all with opportunities for learning and knowledge integration. Knowing and understanding the continuum of writing skills and how one skill facilitates the development of the next skill helps you build a progression that offers clear distinctions between levels of writing, making writing growth more visible, explainable, and consequently, more achievable. When you can create these sorts of successful experiences, working from students' ZPD, you reinforce the joy and curiosity that come with learning, and, in turn, you increase confidence and competence.

Great Resources

- Meehan, M. (2019). *Every child can write, grades 2–5: Entry points, bridges, and pathways for striving writers*. Corwin.

- Serravallo, J. (2017). *The writing strategies book*. Heinemann.

- Shubitz, S., & Dorfman, L. (2019). *Welcome to writing workshop*. Stenhouse.

What Are the Different Choices and Models I Have for Instruction?

When my daughters were learning to swim, the instructors demonstrated some of the strokes to a large group when the children were sitting away from the water. After the demonstration, they divided the group, and one instructor took two to four children to various parts of the pool. Students who were especially nervous or scared had a one-to-one instructor until they gained confidence. By the end of the session, almost every child learned to swim.

The structure of these swimming lessons reminds me of the choices and models available for writing instruction. Whole group instruction may sometimes feel chaotic since there are students at either end of the learning spectrum who may not understand or engage as fully as other students. However, if you keep your whole group instruction short relative to your writing block, there will be opportunities to meet with small groups and individual students, as well, allowing for opportunities to address those all important ZPDs. Let's go over the options.

Whole group instruction: Consists of a single teaching point or objective and delivered to the entire class

Small group instruction: Delivered to groups of two to six students based on the learning needs and goals of those students. May be given for a variety of reasons and students can be a heterogeneous mix.

Individual instruction: Also known as conferring, focuses on one student and their individualized learning need or goal

---

WHOLE GROUP INSTRUCTION

Think of whole group instruction as just that—a lesson you deliver to the entire class that follows the trajectory of a unit. While it is efficient to teach one objective to everyone at the same time, realistically, there will be some students at both ends of the spectrum who already know and understand the concept and others who are not ready to learn it. Every whole group lesson should follow a similar structure: introduction, teaching point, active engagement, and link (or what you want students to walk away with).

As you think about whole group instruction, it's easy to envision a lecture or a lengthy explanation. However, 10 minutes is about the maximum for attention spans (Cozolino, 2013). Therefore, think of whole group instruction as a ten-minute instructional period of one specific skill or strategy. Once you deliver that instruction, then students can have opportunities to practice through their own writing.

John Hattie is an Australian education researcher whose meta-studies examine what impacts student learning, influencing many decisions in schools around the world. His research has repeatedly found teacher clarity to be one of the highest impact practices for student learning (Fisher et al., 2019; Hattie, 2011; Hattie et al., 2016). Teacher clarity involves clearly communicating the intentions of the lesson, as well as how students will demonstrate success (Corwin Visible Learning Meta, 2021). If you can fill in the blank, "Today I am going to teach you _____," then you are on the right track. And it's even better for your students if you can fill in the phrase "so that _____" at the end of your learning statement.

Examples of clearly stated teaching points:

- Today I am going to teach you/you are going to learn some options for planning your information pieces so that your writing stays organized as you draft.
- Today I am going to teach you/you are going to learn how to use paragraphs so that it's easier for your readers to understand changes in speakers, settings, or time frames.
- Today I am going to teach you/you are going to learn some transitional phrases you can use as you write your opinion pieces so that your writing flows better for readers.

There is a difference between saying "today I'm going to teach you," and "today you're going to learn," and it's important to pay attention to that difference. The first puts the expectation on the teacher, and putting the expectation on the teacher may take agency and responsibility away from students. However, the second implies that the expectation is on students to learn, even if that learning doesn't always happen. The more you communicate the expectation that students learn and you combine that expectation with clear learning intentions, the more impact your instruction is likely to have.

You have some options as you think about your whole group instruction, still staying far away from a stand-and-deliver or lecture model:

- When you use **demonstration** to deliver a teaching point, you tell students what the teaching point or learning objective is, and you show them how you do it, cueing them to watch and notice how you weave the skill into your writing.
- An **explanation and example** method for teaching allows you to show students where you've used the skill. This method is also useful when you are using any sort of mentor or exemplar texts (see Chapter 1), explaining or envisioning how you made the decision to use and implement the skill.
- An **inquiry** lesson invites the whole group of students to contemplate a question and suggest responses. You might expand or explain some of the responses as students provide them. While it's not a review per se, an inquiry lesson requires students to have some background knowledge to give meaningful responses to the question you're posing.

Type of Teaching Method	Phrases to Use	Reasons for Using	Examples
Demonstration	• Watch me as I . . . • Did you notice as I . . . • Now it's your turn to try . . . • As you work on your own writing, go ahead and try . . .	To deliver a clear teaching point	Watch me as I: • Change paragraphs in my story • Use transitional language to explain my reason
Explanation and example	• Today I want to teach you/you will learn about . . . • I tried that here/I noticed _____ tried that here . . . • Here's how I did that/how I bet ___ did that . . . • Let's think about the steps or the process so that you can try it in your own writing.	To introduce students to strategies To demonstrate decision-making within writing	Today you will learn about • Ways to bring characters to life in your story • How to break up lists in your information writing
Inquiry	• I have a question for you to consider: ___ • What are some possible ways to answer this question? • As you work on your writing, think about the choices and options you have as writers and use those.	To challenge students to contemplate a question and suggest responses	What are some possible ways to • Hook readers at the beginning of your pieces? • End your piece so that readers remember and care about your topic?

Keep in Mind

An inquiry lesson will fall flat if students are unable to come up with any responses to the question you're posing. If this happens as you're teaching, be prepared to shift to a demonstration or explanation/ example model.

TIMING YOUR LESSON

Ten minutes is the recommended timeframe for your initial instruction for several reasons. First, there is brain research that suggests elementary students are able to pay attention for 7–10 minutes. Also, students need to practice any skill they are learning. With 45–60 minutes typically devoted to writing, you need to make sure there is enough time to practice, a key component of effective writing instruction (Graham, 2008; Graham, 2019; Graves, 2003). To stay under that magic 10-minute mark, it helps to establish a structure. While you don't always have to follow an exact framework, it helps to have predictability both for you and for students. The gradual release model—or "I do, we do, you do"—is a framework that grounds many lessons (Fisher & Frey, 2008), and you can think about it when you plan a whole group lesson. The following chart may help you establish the consistent routine and structure of a whole group lesson.

Length of Time	What You Might Be Doing or Saying	Example	Rationale
Introduction: 1 minute	Tell a story that somehow relates to the lesson or reminds students of what they have learned and how this skill fits into the sequence of learning.	If the lesson is about introductions, tell about how the announcer introduced players and welcomed fans to last night's athletic event.	This sort of beginning gets students' attention because it shares an aspect of your life and lets them know what the lesson is about.
Teaching point: 5–7 minutes	State the learning goal and then show students ways to do that. During this time, it's best to have a "no question" policy because questions can extend the time you have for capitalizing on attention spans.	Using a demonstration piece of writing, show three different ways to make an introduction interesting. This is a time to use visual support such as a chart to support student learning.	This is the "I do" part of the lesson where you explicitly and intentionally show students how to do the skill.
Active engagement: 2–3 minutes	Offer students a chance to try out the skill, envision the skill in their own writing, or talk about how they could use it.	Students could turn and talk to each other about which strategy they will try in their own introduction and how it might go.	Setting goals is important for learning (Marzano, 2009), and making choices about learning leads to engagement (Parker et al., 2017); this is when students are invited to make decisions about their work. It is the "we do" part of the lesson.
Link: 1 minute	Make sure that students understand that this skill should now be part of their repertoire.	If you are co-creating an anchor chart with students—and I hope you are!—this is when you'd direct students to that chart so they know where and how to find how to write an introduction.	Not everyone should be at the same place at the same time because writers create different lengths and at different paces. Therefore, you want to make sure they know where to look and how to access information when they're ready. This part of the lesson is explicitly moving students into the "you do" part of the lesson.

Once you are finished with your whole group lesson, students should have time for independent writing. During this time, students should be working on their own pieces, practicing their growing repertoire of skills. While they are working on their own, you should have time for small group instruction and conferring with individual students.

DIRECT INSTRUCTION VERSUS INQUIRY

When you are in a direct instruction mode, you state the teaching point, demonstrate how it looks in practice, and provide a short amount of time for students to interact with the concept. If you are moving into an inquiry lesson, then you pose a question and invite students to provide answers to the question. Students should know enough about the concept to be able to provide responses.

Direct Instruction	Inquiry
• There is a clear teaching point/learning objective that is stated as a sentence. • The teacher provides direct instruction about the objective. • Students may know little to nothing about the objective. • Example: Today I'm going to teach you/ you will learn about the different ways and reasons writers use commas as they write.	• The learning objective is stated as a question. • Students provide responses that answer the question. • Students should know enough about the topic to provide answers to the question. • Example: What are the different ways and reasons for using commas?

When done effectively, an inquiry lesson is engaging for students because it invites participation. However, if you plan an inquiry, pose a question, and then get not much in the way of quality responses, you need to be ready to shift right back to direct instruction.

While an inquiry lesson is related to inquiry-based learning, it is different. Inquiry-based learning involves a process where students identify a question or topic to explore based on their own interest and curiosity, they research, and then they present or take action. An inquiry lesson asks students for ideas around a question that relates to a teaching point or learning objective.

Examples of inquiry lessons within writing instruction:

- What are some different ways writers can plan their stories?
- What are ways writers can hook readers at the beginning of their stories/ information pieces/opinion essays?
- What tools do writers have to help them write their best?

To answer the question you pose, students may tap into their own knowledge and understanding, expand and elaborate through collaborating and listening to each other, or explore resources such as mentor texts. However, if you find yourself in the middle of an inquiry lesson and no one is able to provide answers or ideas that support learning, then you'll want to shift to a model of direct instruction, as described in the previous section.

SMALL GROUP INSTRUCTION

Julie Wright (2018), co-author of *What Are You Grouping For?* and educational consultant, calls small group instruction the sweet spot of instruction. Using small group instruction is powerful because you can be efficient while meeting the learning needs and challenges of everyone you're teaching at the same time. Both small group instruction and individual conferring, which is covered in the next section, should happen as a direct result of reading and responding to their writing. When reading student writing, work to develop your lens of assessment. Does the writing contain a clear structure? Is the writer using a variety of elaboration strategies? By considering the traits of writing and keeping in mind a progression for the development of those traits, you will increase the effectiveness of both small group instruction and individual conferences.

Small group instruction can take many forms and serve many functions. While there is no one right way, it's important to determine goals for small groups. Any type of small group experience should engage your students and nudge them toward independence. Your decisions impact how you plan and deliver small group instruction.

Some questions to think about include:

- What will be the big takeaways for students engaged in this small group?
- How long will the group stay together?
- Who will be in charge of the learning and outcomes that happen as a result of this small group work?

Small group instruction is a powerful way to address specific learning objectives that benefit a small number of students in the classroom. If your small group instruction is aimed at a specific learning objective or outcome, then small group instruction may follow similar formats and protocols as whole group instruction, except that you can use small group instruction to differentiate and target students' learning readiness. When delivering a whole group lesson, you may well have students on either end of the readiness spectrum, but when delivering a small group lesson, if you are assessing, organizing, and planning, then everyone should be learning something that is relevant and timely for where they are at that moment.

Just as whole group instruction has an architecture, so does small group instruction, and it can be similar to the Timing Your Lesson chart shown in the whole group instruction segment. However, there are times when I have less of an introduction and begin with a statement along the lines of "I'm pulling you together because _____." Depending on how you decide on and plan for small group instruction, students may already know why they're being pulled together because they've been part of a goal-setting process (see Chapter 5).

HOW TO FORM SMALL GROUPS

While groups of students can be formed based on common strengths or weaknesses as determined by student writing or some other form of assessment, not all students in a small group lesson need to be at the same level as they work on that skill. For example, it could be they are all working on a catchy lead for an informational introduction. The levels of writing might be different, but the strategies can be similar. Some ways to form groups include:

1   Do a quick sort of student writing and ask yourself what teaching point would help these students. When just starting out, it's helpful to think in terms of categories such as:

- Structure
- Development
- Conventions
- Stamina
- Generating
- Elaboration skills
- Planning

2   Ask students to set goals. You can start with some ideas for them, as you may get a lot of blank faces when you first make the suggestion. Here are a few to get a classroom of writers thinking about goals during a narrative writing unit:

- Having a clear beginning, middle, and end
- Using transitional phrases to help readers follow what is going on
- Balancing dialogue with description and action
- Including thinking within writing
- Stretching out important parts

3   Have students sign up for seminars. When students analyze their own work and set goals for themselves, you can ask them to communicate those goals. One way for them to do that is to sign up for seminars, a process that is described more thoroughly in Chapter 5.

When planning small group instruction, you will want to think about not only what the learning objective will be but also how long the group will stay together. You may want to set up a series of small group lessons with the same group of students. This structure creates accountability and inspires students to approximate and work on a specific skill since you've set the expectation that you, as well as the other students in the group, will be coming back together to check on the progress. If students understand and expect that the focus of the small group sessions will span over the course of a week or two, their sustained attention should lead to even more intentional practice for longer than just a class period. The following chart shows what this could look like:

Example of How a Series of Small Group Lessons Could Go	
Skill	**Plan**
Bringing character to life with dialogue	Session 1: Use demonstration writing to show both contextual dialogue and speech bubbles.
	Session 2: Check in with students to see that they are trying it out, nudging them to try both strategies if they haven't already.
	Session 3: Invite students to share how they've used dialogue, evaluating the effectiveness of it within each other's writing.

Mastery rarely happens through one day of practice, and a series of small group instruction has the power to maintain students' focus on new learning.

While the first two questions lean into what skills you'll address and for how many sessions, the third question has more to do with who directs the small group work. Small group work can be an opportunity for students to take initiative and increase their agency over their own learning. One way is to ask students to sign up for seminars that address a specific skill. The concept of a seminar can be inspiring in and of itself since it suggests a high-level learning opportunity. This movement toward student directedness will be addressed more in Chapter 5. Students can also offer seminars, and teaching a skill is a great way for students to achieve mastery. "One of the quickest ways to learn something new, and to practice it, is to teach others how to do it," Amy Gallo (2012) reminds us.

Both questions that pertain to length of time and who's in charge bring up the possibilities of students creating something as a result of small group work. In writing, they may create a shared piece of text, representative of multiple contributions. They may also take on different roles in a process. This sort of small group work opens up possibilities for efficiency and collaboration, important skills across content areas.

Great Resources

- Diller, D. (2021). *Simply small groups: Differentiating literacy learning in any setting.* Corwin.

- Serravallo, J. (2021). *Teaching writing in small groups.* Heinemann.

- Wright, J. T., & Hoonan, B. (2018). *What are you grouping for? How to guide small groups based on readers—not the book.* Corwin.

WHEN TO DELIVER SMALL GROUP INSTRUCTION

Students can be brought together while the rest of the class is working independently, and the teacher should be clear about the reason for bringing them together. Just as a teacher states the teaching point during whole group instruction, a teacher should state the teaching point during small group instruction. In fact, many times the format should follow the architecture of whole group instruction with the teaching point, the active engagement, and the link. While students are practicing the new skill, the teacher may even have time to walk away from them and have a conference with another student.

In any type of small group instruction, remember that less is usually more. If you teach them one thing and their writing changes, you've accomplished more than if you teach them several things and nothing changes.

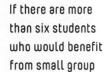

Keep in Mind

If there are more than six students who would benefit from small group instruction, then consider making it a whole group lesson.

Agency and Identity

Small group instruction should involve students collaborating about what they will try and how it might look in their work. Try to keep small group instruction at an even number of students. That way, students can partner to try out or talk about a teaching point.

INDIVIDUALIZED INSTRUCTION OR CONFERRING

Individualized instruction, also known as **conferring**, is when a teacher works one to one with a student. The more conversational the conference can be, the better, because conferring is an opportunity to get to know students as people, as well as teach them something as writers.

Following a structure helps keep the conference short and streamlined. The more you can stick to a predictable structure for your conference, the more efficient and effective you will become. Remember the structure for a conference and use that with as much fidelity as you can! A format that may help you keep your conferences efficient could be:

- Researching/reading: You'll need to take time to read a student's writing and decide what single focus your instruction will center on.
- Compliment or noticing: Specifically naming something the student is doing is feedback, and effective feedback correlates to higher learning rates (Hattie, 2011).
- Teaching point: Just as you taught in whole group and small group instruction, you'll want to teach and demonstrate the objective.
- Challenge: As you leave the student, you'll want to challenge them to continue to try the strategy without you by their side.

 ### Equity and Access

Some students may take longer to settle into their work, and students' processing speeds may vary as well. Don't be in a hurry to decide on what to teach a student right away. You can take your time reading and getting to know the writer. This is time well spent since knowing students is an important component of culturally responsive teaching!

Individual conferences should take 5–10 minutes. When you maintain your focus on one teaching point in the conference, it's easier to stay within that amount of time. Keep in mind the importance of clarity as you confer. The more students know what you are teaching and what they should be learning, the more effective the instruction is likely to be. Additionally, your efficiency with conferring will increase as students learn and take on their roles and responsibilities. I make it a routine to ask students what I've taught them and to have them explain it to me in their own words. When they expect that question, they listen differently, and they're ready to answer! However, their active participation takes practice, and until they understand their role, I sometimes have to repeat instruction, and that takes extra time. Students frequently do not listen or remember the compliment you give, and the positive feedback of what they're doing well has the potential to increase the learning curve. Say ahead of time, "I'm giving you a compliment." Once you do, ask the student to repeat the compliment in their own words.

The conference cards shown in Figure 3.3 help streamline the flow of a conference. The pink card is designed for the teacher to fill out, although I ask students what I should write for both the compliment and the teaching point. The blue card shifts more responsibility to the student, and the expectation for that card is that the student fills it out.

Figure 3.3 Conference cards are powerful artifacts to fill out and leave with students.

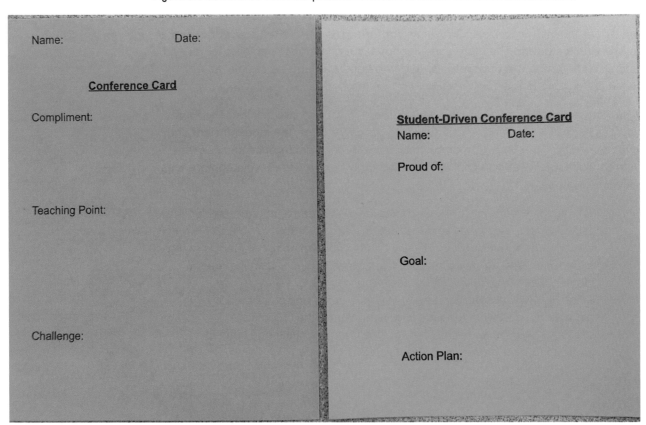

 Keep in Mind

It's time well spent to pause and record what you've worked on with students during a conference. No matter how well-intentioned you are, it's difficult to remember compliments and teaching points if you wait until the end of the day to maintain your records.

To prepare for individual conferences, you will want to develop a toolkit of sorts. If you have a few go-to charts that address structure, development, and conventions, you will be able to address many of the issues you'll find as you read over students' shoulders. You'll want to get in the habit of taking pictures of charts you make with students (see Chapter 1), and then you can print those pictures. Having small versions on hand is invaluable as you sit next to students for individualized instruction. Additionally, knowing one or two mentor texts well will help you have the tools you need. It's also helpful to have conferring cards or even blank cardstock on hand. As you confer more and more, your toolkit will grow and you'll become more and more comfortable creating tools and resources that reflect your teaching.

Tools to Have on Hand for Small Group Instruction and Individual Conferring

- A range of mentor texts that illustrate specific teaching points

- Samples of student writing

- Blank paper and markers to give a quick lesson on the fly

- Miniature charts of specific strategies that can be given to the students

Great Resources

- Anderson, C. (2018). *A teacher's guide to writing conferences.* Heinemann.

- TwoWritingTeachers.org is a blog with many posts and ideas about conferring with students.

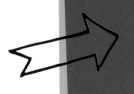

How Should I Balance Whole Group Instruction With Small Group and Individualized Instruction?

Consider that whole group instruction will meet the learning needs of about 50% to 75% of students at that moment in time. Therefore, you definitely don't want to spend too high of a percentage of time on it! Your whole group lesson should take 8 to 12 minutes and should introduce a skill or concept that students will practice over time. Don't expect every child to immediately understand and apply what you've taught in the whole group.

MANAGE AND MAXIMIZE YOUR TIME

Small group instruction is your most efficient way of differentiating because it should focus on a skill that all participants are working on. You want to make sure that your small group instruction stays focused on the stated objective and doesn't become a session for individual teaching points. If you are in the middle of a small group session and you realize that one student is not as ready for a skill as you thought they'd be, consider sending that student back to independent writing and schedule an individual conference.

Pay attention and self-monitor the amount of time you spend with each student in a conference and how often you work with individual students. A conference should take about five to ten minutes. If you find yourself spending longer than that, or if you are meeting with the same student daily, then you may need to adjust what you are asking them to do.

 Equity and Access

Any small group or individual teaching point should be able to be practiced and approximated by the student right away. If a student continues to need guidance and direction to use the skill, then it could be the student is not ready for that lesson or skill.

One way to push yourself toward efficient differentiation practice is to consider the blocks of time in your writing class. If you have a 20-minute block of independent writing time, set a goal to have one small group session, one partner session, and one individual session. If you have two independent blocks, then you could be differentiating for up to 14 students a session! Realistically, if you get to one small group and a few conferences, you're still meeting the learning needs of several students a day.

Figure 3.4 shows how much relative time to spend in each portion of your writing block.

Answers to Your Biggest Questions About Teaching Elementary Writing

Figure 3.4 A writing class should consist of both instructional time and daily opportunities for independent practice.

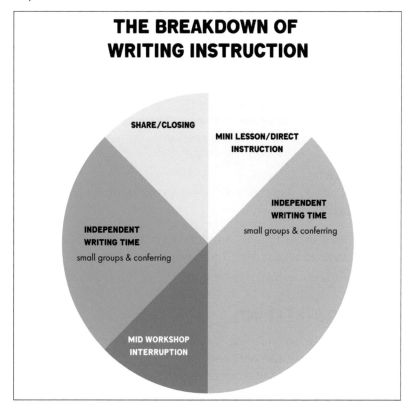

KEEP RECORDS OF YOUR INSTRUCTION

As you develop your instructional practices, you will meet with several students on any given day. Record-keeping is one of those tedious chores that seems to take away from the time you spend with students but is a critical component of your practice, helping you see the tracks of your teaching and hold students accountable for trying out, approximating, and moving toward mastery of what they are learning.

Additionally, record-keeping helps you distribute your time equitably among your students, ensuring that you are not spending an inordinate amount of time with the same students, an easy trap to fall into.

There are many systems and structures that you can set up, and you'll want to find the one that works for you. Here are a few ideas to get you started.

ANALOG RECORD-KEEPING

PAPER CHARTS ON CLIPBOARDS
This analog system works well for many teachers! To keep track of conferences, I recommend a record-keeping sheet that could be structured as follows:

Goals:			
Child's Name/Date	Research/ Compliment	Teaching Point	What's Next for This Student?

How Should I Balance Whole Group Instruction With Small Group and Individualized Instruction?

83

To keep track of small group instruction, a document that could be structured as followed works well:

Small Group Instruction			
Date	Students' Names	Teaching Point	What's Next?

Both documents can be single pages, and they allow you to take quick notes as you meet with students during a single writing session.

A BINDER SYSTEM

Stickers are a great option, especially if more than one adult is meeting with students in your classroom.

Set up a system where each student has a tab in a binder, and use address sticky notes or address labels to take notes. That way, you can transfer the notes right into the students' sections.

DIGITAL RECORD-KEEPING

There are many options for digital note-taking! You can set up systems using Google Forms with pre-filled-out compliments and teaching points. These digital systems are especially efficient because you can check off several students at the same time if you are teaching a small group. Otherwise, you have to take separate notes for each student who was involved in a small group.

Search the internet for "record-keeping for writing instruction," and you will find many ideas for keeping track of your teaching. The system you choose must fit your style and needs, however, because to be effective and have positive impact on student learning, every idea requires you to take the time to take those notes and then use them to inform your instruction. You will find that this time is worth it! The best record-keeping system is the one you'll stick with.

ESTABLISH AND MAINTAIN TRANSITIONS THAT MAXIMIZE INSTRUCTION

Routines are important because students should be able to transition from attending to lessons and independent work without much wasted time. Consider spending time teaching students what an effective transition looks like. The lesson could go something like this:

Today I'm going to teach you how to shift from my lesson to your independent work. When I finish the lesson, I will ask for questions from individuals while the rest of you get started on writing. To get started, you will need to:

- Clear your work area of anything you do not need for writing.
- Make sure that you have what you DO need. (This will vary from class to class and even from student to student. You might want to list what it is that students need.)
- Reread what you wrote from the previous writing session and establish a work plan for yourself for today's writing block.
- Get started.

Source: Meehan (2019).

How Should I Balance Whole Group Instruction With Small Group and Individualized Instruction?

85

INSTRUCTION

What Are the Roles of Both Teacher and Students Within Writing Instruction?

The better students understand both your role as their teacher and their role as active participants in their own learning processes, the more effective your writing instruction will be, so it's worth taking the time to teach or review the concepts of roles and responsibilities. If you know that you have a regular one-hour block of time, you might divide it into whole group instruction with time for independent practice and more targeted instruction. You can choose an instructional model and deliver a lesson on what you and students should be doing during any and all parts of a writing instructional block.

ROLES DURING WHOLE GROUP INSTRUCTION

When you are delivering a whole group lesson, your responsibility is to state the learning goal and teach it or demonstrate it with clarity and efficiency. I find myself saying during this time that it's my turn to talk and asking students to hold their questions. Once the instructional five to seven minutes is over, students should have time to try out the skill or discuss it. When they do that, they should have paid enough attention to the lesson that they are able to! Ideally, they are paying attention like an apprentice, with the intention that they will be trying it out in their own writing.

Roles During Whole Group Instruction	
Teacher Role	**Student Role**
Deliver a clear learning objective with demonstration or explanation in under 10 minutes	Listen and try it out Create some sort of artifact or system for remembering the lesson

ROLES DURING INDEPENDENT WRITING TIME

Imagine a writing classroom where you are able to meet with small groups of students, as well as individuals, while the rest of the class is writing and problem-solving independently without interrupting you or disrupting each other. This scenario happens when students understand their roles during independent writing time. During this time, if they are not meeting with you, then they should be working on their piece, using tools and resources that are available to them, or talking to each other about their work and process. For this to happen, you'll need to have created charts (see Chapter 1), introduced mentor texts (see Chapters 1 and 2), and taught how to be effective writing partners (see the next section). As students internalize the usefulness of those components, you will reap the benefits of a more and more productive independent writing time. You may get to a point when you look around and feel like you're not sure what to do because everyone is working so effectively!

Roles During Independent Writing Time	
Teacher Role	**Student Role**
Meet with small groups and individual students to provide targeted instruction Make sure that students have resources that they know how to access and use to nurture independence	Work on independent writing pieces Use or create tools and resources that build independence Meet with each other to ask questions or offer suggestions about each other's writing

Agency and Identity

One of my favorite strategies to use during independent writing time is to ask students to take inventory, self-assessing their productivity right at the moment that I interrupt with the phrase, "Writers, take inventory: How on task are you right now?" Students can indicate with their fingers their level of productivity where one finger indicates "not so much" and five fingers indicates "about as good as it gets." This strategy can become a routine that helps students self-assess and self-monitor their own engagement and productivity.

ROLES DURING SMALL GROUP OR INDIVIDUAL INSTRUCTION

Many of the roles and responsibilities of whole group instruction remain the same for both teachers and students when the groups are smaller. The teacher is still responsible for planning and delivering instruction with clarity and efficiency. Students' roles are even more active because the instruction is so responsive to their learning needs. Additionally, because the lesson should be challenging for the students, they should try out the new concepts with the expectation that they'll make progress, but not achieve instant mastery or perfection. The reminder of never allowing perfect to get in the way of progress is especially relevant during small group and individual instruction.

Roles During Small Group and Individual Instruction	
Teacher Role	**Student Role**
Deliver a clear learning objective with demonstration or explanation that is responsive to the small group or individual learners Provide resources or artifacts for students to use or create to aid in their internalization and transfer of the teaching point	Listen and learn with the understanding that the lesson is specifically tailored for them Ask clarifying questions as needed Try out the new learning with the expectation of progress and not perfection

As with many lessons, whether they relate to skills, process, or behavior, you can think about this lesson through the lens of direct instruction or inquiry.

Direct Instruction	Inquiry Question
Today you will learn the roles we both have throughout the different parts of writing class.	What are the roles of the teacher and students throughout our writing class?

Regardless of your teaching decision, make sure you carve out the time for it. When students know their roles and take responsibility for their learning, you will increase the progress they make as writers.

Notes

What Resources Do I Need for High-Impact Instruction, and How Do I Introduce Them?

Resources should consider and build independence. Charts serve as instructional artifacts, and they can remind students of what they have learned, as well as how to complete tasks. Mentor texts are also powerful resources for students to access for independent learning. You might offer a lesson along the lines of "Today you will learn about some of the tools and resources you can use for your own learning when I am working with other people." Classmates also become resources as you establish productive writing partnerships.

INTENTIONAL CLASSROOM CHARTS

Charts are helpful for visual learners and as a learning trail for students who may benefit from a reminder on another day. The more that students see charts as tools and resources that help them when you're not available, the more learning opportunities those students have. If you create an "interactive" bulletin board such as the one shown in Figure 3.6, with clearly labeled pocket charts full of tools students can use, then you can teach students to take what they need *when* they need it.

Figure 3.6 This bulletin board is set up to provide charts students can take and use at their desks when they feel the charts are necessary or helpful.

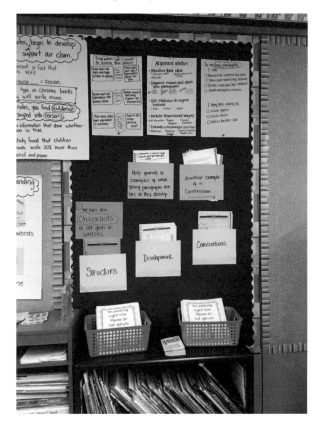

Many teachers feel pressure to have beautiful charts, but charts do not need to be perfect to be effective. Students will understand charts much more if you create the chart in front of—or better yet—*with* them. When you create charts with your students, you co-create, share the ownership of the classroom, and set the stage for higher levels of learning.

Equity and Access

Students should know how, where, and when to access resources for independent learning so that there is never a line at the teacher's desk for help.

MENTOR AUTHORS AND TEXTS

Stacey Shubitz (2016) writes in *Craft Moves*,

> Authors are like trusted colleagues we invite to teach alongside us. Their books inspire us, their personal stories and struggles resonate with us, and they show us new ways of understanding. We welcome authors we trust into our classrooms to help us teach our students strategies that will help them become better writers. (p. 15)

Shubitz refers to mentor authors; there is a difference between mentor authors and mentor texts, and both can help build independence and inspiration in your writing classroom. Mentor authors become people students think of as they write. Meg Medina inspires writers to bring repetition, figurative language, and other poetic techniques into their pieces since these elements exist in so many of her books.

Meg Medina's books to use for inspiration:

- Medina, M. (2020a). *Evelyn Del Rey is moving away.* Candlewick Press.
- Medina, M. (2020b). *Tía Isa wants a car.* Candlewick Press.
- Medina, M. (2021). *Mango, abuela, and me.* Candlewick Press.

Jacqueline Woodson has written many picture books and chapter books that inspire writers. She shares about her process and the books' development on her website, https://www.jacquelinewoodson.com/category/books-ive-written/picture-books/, and these reflections make her that much more of a powerful mentor author for students. Many other authors share generous insights and reflections about their writing lives; when you have students who gravitate toward specific authors, do a little online exploring to see if that author offers some mentoring advice.

Mentor texts are singular works by an author that illustrate concepts students are working on as writers. Mentor texts can be picture books, chapter books, parts of an anthology, magazine contributions, or even unpublished texts, as long as they contain craft moves that students can notice, name, and approximate in their own writing.

Keep in Mind

You will notice that I talk about approximation throughout this book. Writing is rarely about mastery. It's more about experimentation and attempts. I've never heard an author say that they wrote a first-draft masterpiece, and the more you can build the mindset of trying out moves and revision, the stronger the writers you are likely to have in your classroom.

Using mentor texts involves a process. Before using any piece of writing as a writer, you'll want to experience it as a reader. After reading it, you can begin to notice and name the craft moves.

Keep in mind the importance of doing the work yourself, both so you can consider the cognitive processes that it involves and also create the powerful message for students that you are a writer. Like many, I am sometimes guilty of skipping the crucial step of modeling how I use a mentor text to inspire my own writing. Read the piece, read it again, and notice the craft move, name the craft move, and *try* the craft move yourself as head learner in your classroom. Students need to see what it looks like to try it out. They need to see the process of revision or interpretation of a craft move. Do not let perfect get in the way of the good because seeing the process, especially if it's a little hard and doesn't go perfectly, gives students more courage to be brave writers and experiment with new skills. Courage is an important ingredient for growth.

Great Resources

- Mentor Text Charts: This Google link (https://bit.ly/3kHpN03) contains a collection of charts I have made for specific picture books and information texts. Because many picture books are not paginated, I start the page numbers on the first page of written text.

- Dorfman, L. R., Cappelli, R., & Hoyt, L. (2017). *Mentor texts: Teaching writing through children's literature, K–6*. Stenhouse.

- Koutrakos, P. A. (2022). *Mentor texts that multitask [grades K–8]: A less-is-more approach to integrated literacy instruction*. Corwin.

- Shubitz, S. (2016). *Craft moves: Lesson sets for teaching writing with mentor texts*. Stenhouse.

WRITING TOOLS AND MATERIALS

Writing requires materials, especially for younger grades. Young students should know how and where to access paper, utensils, and anything else you want them to have. You'll want to take the time to teach students how to choose paper, as well as choose and care for writing utensils. Depending on the age, experience, and make-up of the class, you will need to be responsively explicit. You may even need a lesson on how to replace a cap on a pen.

INSTRUCTION

Equity and Access

Paper is a powerful scaffold for writers. Depending on their fluency and volume, you can inspire or frustrate writers by providing paper with too many or too few lines. Offer choices of paper for elementary students. The number of lines can vary, as well as the size and placements of picture boxes.

Paper has the power to deliver important messages to young writers. Too few lines may hold writers back since they may fill lines and feel like they're done. In contrast, too many lines may overwhelm writers since blank pages can feel scary when you're not sure how to get started and the process is not yet fluent or fluid. Sometimes wide lines lead to messy handwriting, and sometimes narrow lines are inhibiting for students who are working on fine motor skills. Challenge yourself to find the just right number of lines for individual students with the same mindset that you establish zones of proximal development. The right number of lines for a student is the number that feels just at the edge of comfort.

WRITER'S NOTEBOOKS

Many students are ready to experiment with a writer's notebook by the time they are in third grade, while for some it may be earlier, and for others it may be later. *Rules* and *systems* are not set in stone but are rather practices that teach, inspire, and energize young writers to notice, collect, and celebrate before making decisions about bringing pieces to life outside of their notebooks.

If you think of notebooks as both workbenches and playgrounds, you'll help students understand when to use notebooks and when to bring their work outside of them. A good rule of thumb is that once writers are ready to draft, they leave the notebook pages and work on paper or a device. Notebooks can be filled with stories, reactions, ideas, photos, news clippings, poems, a napkin with writing when there was no access to paper, favorite words, quotes, and more. The more you also keep a notebook and share your own personal connections and the significance of *why* your notebook is important, the better for students.

I recommend teaching an explicit lesson of what goes in a notebook and what does not, although the rules, inclusions, and exclusions are not rigid.

 *Keep in Mind*

If students aren't using notebooks effectively, they might not be ready for them. Effective notebook writers require fluency; if it's still a struggle for writers to get words down on pages, then consider moving them back to paper for their entire writing process.

What Goes in a Writer's Notebook	What Doesn't Go in Writer's Notebook
• Ideas and lists • Favorite lines or quotes • Sketches • Strategies, notes, and tricks for remembering • Plans • Different or experimental ways a piece could go • Punctuation	• Elaborate drawings • Torn pages (especially ones caused by too much erasing!) • Drafting • Perfection!

Composition books work well for students' writer's notebooks, and you'll want to have students decorate the outside of them with pictures, stickers, quotes, or anything else they find inspiring. This decorating process leads to ownership of their notebooks, and it also becomes a resource when students are stuck for ideas. Most pictures have stories behind them!

Great Resources

Books have been written about writer's notebooks, as well as countless posts. Here are a few favorites:

- Buckner, A. E. (2005). *Notebook know-how: Strategies for the writer's notebook.* Stenhouse.

- Fletcher, R. J. (2003). *A writer's notebook: Unlocking the writer within you.* HarperTrophy.

- Hubbard, B. (2018, November 12). ICYMI: Notebooks as a writer's tool. *Two Writing Teachers.* https://bit.ly/3ozxEOG

WRITING PARTNERSHIPS

Every professional writer I know has a writing friend or a group who encourages and supports them throughout the process. Partnerships in writing class have the potential to empower students and build an authentic writing environment. As you think about introducing partnerships to your classroom, there are a few considerations that will strengthen their impact.

Invite students into the choosing process:

Have students create "Writing Partner Wanted" posters, like the one pictured. These posters can be personalized, and they can also be differentiated depending on the grade. You might brainstorm different traits and categories before asking students to create their own poster and emphasize to them the importance of prioritizing their preferences.

Figure 3.7 Students should think about what matters to them when it comes to a writing partner.

What Resources Do I Need for High-Impact Instruction, and How Do I Introduce Them?

93

Have students create T-charts of what they'd like in a writing partner and what they can offer, as pictured in Figure 3.8. Before students can really do this work, they should understand some of the grade-level expectations for writing traits and behaviors. I recommend spending some time teaching those before asking students to create this sort of T-chart.

Figure 3.8 Students can think about what they would like and what they would offer writing partners.

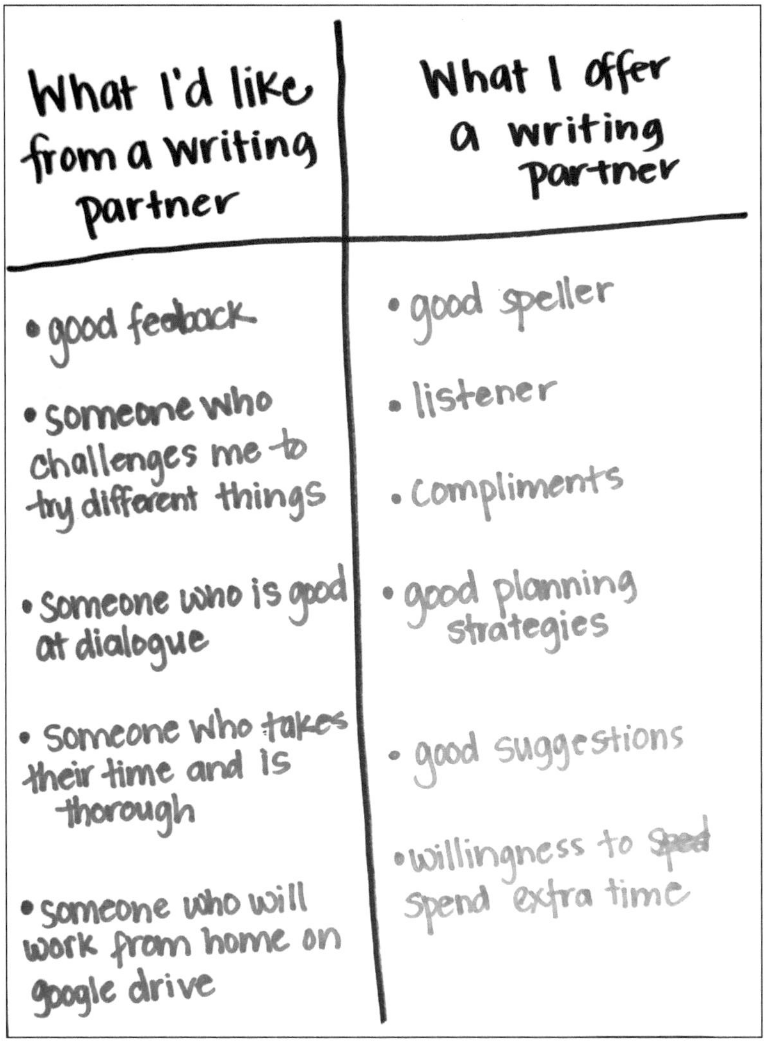

What I'd like from a writing partner	What I offer a writing partner
• good feedback	• good speller
• someone who challenges me to try different things	• listener
• someone who is good at dialogue	• compliments
• someone who takes their time and is thorough	• good planning strategies
• someone who will work from home on google drive	• good suggestions
	• willingness to spend extra time

> ## Some Dos and Don'ts About Setting Up Writing Partnerships
>
> DO:
>
> - Commit to these partnerships being in place for a while—at least for the unit, and possibly longer.
>
> - Allow some partnerships to remain in place even when others switch. A strong partnership is a gift!
>
> - Teach into how writing partners choose each other and what they might look for.
>
> - Pay attention to students' input about setting up partnerships.
>
> - Be ready to teach into successful partnership behavior.
>
> DON'T:
>
> - Worry about having same-sex partnerships. Boys and girls work really well together as writing partners in workshops.
>
> - Be in a rush to set them up. Waiting to see how the writing community evolves for two to three weeks is fine!
>
> - Have writing partnerships be the same as reading partnerships.
>
> - Try to pair strong writers with struggling writers. Your strong writers will benefit by having peers who will push them, and your struggling writers may find inspiration and confidence when they work with people who are close to their own levels or working on similar skills.

Writing partnerships are an important element of workshop instruction, but one that requires careful planning and instruction. The investment of time in this area to establish successful, productive, independent partnerships is incredibly worthwhile!

 Equity and Access

>   If you have a student who misses writing class on a regular basis for any reason, consider having that student be a member of a triad rather than a twosome. That way, there are opportunities for the other students to engage in partnership work and to include the third student when they are there.

How Do I Balance Approximation and Intentional Practice That Leads to Learning and Mastery?

Writing involves the integration of many skills. And it's important to understand the difference between approximation, or trying to improve a skill, and mastery of that skill.

Equity and Access

If you believe that equity involves high rates of learning for everyone and that learning involves the transfer of skills and concepts to new situations, then there must be agency and independence. Sometimes the transfer of a new skill won't show mastery. You're not looking for perfection; you're looking for progress!

ACCEPT APPROXIMATION VERSUS MASTERY

Let's think about students as they improve their ability to think of stories. Then, they face drafting. They begin to draft, and they have to take on the challenge of adding details. Students start to integrate each skill into their writing, but sometimes they may focus on one skill more than another. Just as athletes practice new skills with intention, developing writers also should be able to say what they are working on. And as they are working on it, they should be showing improvement but not necessarily mastery of every skill.

Approximation: Showing some elements of a skill, but not all

Examples include:

- Periods at the end of every line when a student is learning to use end punctuation
- Quotation marks around when a character is talking, but without the punctuation within the quotation marks
- Overusing similes and figurative language or using ones that aren't relevant or meaningful

Intentional Practice: Working on a skill with the knowledge and understanding of what they are working toward

Mastery: Getting to the place where you can use the skill fluently and accurately

Agency and Identity

An expectation of perfection may be paralyzing to writers, so you may want to adopt a class mantra along the lines of "Don't let perfect get in the way of the good."

CONSIDER COGNITIVE DEMAND

Cognitive demand is an important concept to consider as you think about approximation, intentional practice, and mastery. Cognitive demand is how hard the brain has to work to do something, and there are limits to what we can ask and expect!

I find myself returning to an athletic analogy again here. If I think about a tennis forehand, there are several tips to remember: squeeze the grip, hold the racquet back, step forward, swing low to high, hit the middle of the strings, meet the ball at a specific height depending on the shot. Because I've hit many forehands in my life, these skills are ingrained in my brain and my muscle memory. However, when I am teaching someone or when I'm not playing well, I pick one to focus on and then bring in another once I'm seeing or feeling success.

Asking students to remember and practice everything at once has the potential to be overwhelming. Consider the cognitive demand of each skill—or prioritize according to what's reasonable for each student—so students can feel successful with one or two skills before moving on to practice a third.

As you think about the steps involved in creating a text, think about the impact if one of those steps can't be taken. For example, if a writer can't think of an idea, then how can that writer enter into the realms of planning and drafting? You can work hard at improving idea generation, but sometimes you can also bypass that step, offering a different entry point by providing a topic. Sometimes experiencing success later in the process leads to easier access to the earlier steps.

SHARED WRITING

In early elementary grades, students and teachers share and develop ideas for texts, and teachers scribe. For older students, shared writing can look different. Teachers may use shared writing with a small group of students; the group can come up with an idea and a plan, and then they all can work on a piece collaboratively or individually, depending on where they are on the continuum of gradual release. The piece may not be grammatically or conventionally perfect, but the collaboration empowers a group of students to complete a piece quickly. Additionally, the accountability factor inspires contributors to complete their portions.

In addition to thinking about the number of students working on a piece of shared writing, you can also think about additional opportunities for instruction that may occur both within and outside the writing block. Shared writing is when students and teacher come up with ideas for writing as a group. While shared writing could involve a full genre-based writing text, it could also be part of a morning message, a reflection of learning, or a letter about something.

 Equity and Access

Some students who don't initiate or sustain writing for long periods of time have not had much experience with completing a piece of work. Shared writing provides them with the feeling of completion and ownership, and you can use this positive experience to inspire subsequent experiences.

INTERACTIVE WRITING

Interactive writing is a process by which teachers invite students to write, usually within a demonstration piece, essentially modeling parts of the writing process. Teachers may model writing a topic sentence for an introductory paragraph and students contribute what is included within the writing. Teachers may also ask students to fill in missing words that are sight words or current spelling words. The writing that is produced in interactive writing should be correct.

Keep in Mind

Shared writing and interactive writing both engage students in the writing process. Both are part of a balanced literacy model in primary classrooms. In shared writing, students and teachers collaborate, and the teacher does the scribing. Students and teachers share the pen during interactive writing, and it is frequently used to isolate and practice specific skills.

ISOLATED TASK PRACTICE

One of my daughter's soccer coaches used to set up stations for various skills. He had stations for dribbling, as well as passing, juggling, and trapping. He was not replicating a game situation as much as he was providing opportunities for players to practice targeted skills that they could then use in games. Games required players to put all the skills together.

Let's think about drafting a text as our figurative game day. If, as in soccer, there are many skills to integrate and pull from, then it helps to have had meaningful practice with those skills, sometimes in isolation. Therefore, one of my go-to strategies for writers is setting up practice stations for them, *based on the skills they need.*

For example, Thomas learned how to use dialogue, and his entire story became a string of conversations. I taught him in a conference about ways to blend dialogue with other narrative strategies. Then rather than have him revise his own piece right then and there, I had him practice at the "Ping-Pong Dialogue" station I created (see Figures 3.9a and 3.9b). For many writers, including Thomas, revision is easier when the writing is someone else's, but this activity gave him intentional practice of blending dialogue with action, description, and thinking that he could then use purposefully in his own writing.

Keep in Mind

While a worksheet could provide targeted practice, it's more fun to make practice more playful. Additionally, if you are leaning on worksheets or published materials, then make sure that the targeted skills are relevant to the individual student and that the student understands the purpose for the practice. Nonintentional practice is busywork, and you will not see high learning results.

Ping-Pong Dialogue

"Hi Jared."

"Hi!"

"Come on! Do you want to come and get money with me, so I can buy a puppy?"

"Sure."

"Come on."

"I'll get my bike and you get your bike."

Ping-Pong Dialogue

You have been learning about how to break up dialogue in a story. In this piece of text, the character and his friend are going to go get a puppy, but the author has only used dialogue. Your job is to use action, description, and inner thinking so that this scene makes more sense.

_____

_____

_____

_____

_____

_____

_____

_____

When you can pinpoint a skill for a student, you can create a station. The more responsive the station to the students in your classroom, the more effective your stations are likely to be. Some suggestions from my work in classrooms include, but aren't limited to:

- Replacing vague words with more specific ones
- Using transition words in a paragraph
- Breaking up long sentences into shorter ones
- Using capital letters during the drafting process

Keep in Mind

When I create stations, I do *not* show students writing with incorrect conventions. Instead, I show them pieces with the conventions done correctly, and I ask them to notice the conventions and name the reasons for using them. Then I ask them to create their own piece of writing that demonstrates some of the same rules.

How Do I Balance Scaffolding Student Learning With Building Foundational Skills and Understandings?

Scaffolds by definition are structures that should be removed. At a workshop several years ago, Colleen Cruz made a statement that has stayed with me. When we leave scaffolds up for too long, they are no longer scaffolds. They are permanent structures. Therefore, whenever you put a scaffold in place, you should be able to explain its purpose and your plan for removing it or turning over its responsibility to the student.

Possible Scaffold	Plan for Removing It
Graphic organizer	Teach students how to draw or create their own
Paper with a certain number of lines or booklets	Teach students how to choose their own paper and make their own booklets
A list of sight words that students refer to	Keep the list short enough that students memorize the words and no longer need the list

Graphic organizers are used frequently during writing instruction, and they have the power to keep students focused and organized. A quick Google search provides many options on Pinterest, Teachers Pay Teachers, and other websites. However, students should not spend more time and energy on their organizer than they do on their writing. Furthermore, if you can teach students to create their *own* organizers as opposed to one that is professionally created, then you empower the student.

Instead of . . .	Try this . . .
A picture of a hamburger for an opinion piece where the bun represents the introduction and conclusion and the reasons are the "meat"	Boxes and bullets that students can draw and create themselves
A story mountain where there are a specified number of events for a narrative piece	A student-drawn storyline or mountain with however many events the student decides
A concept map for an informational piece	Teaching students to draw their own squares, representing the amount of information for each one by how large the square is

Answers to Your Biggest Questions About Teaching Elementary Writing

End-of-Chapter Reflections

What might you try within the next week? The next month?

As you consider your instruction, what elements feel strong and secure? What are some elements that you consider opportunities for growth?

What are three goals that you are setting related to instruction?

How Do I Balance Scaffolding Student Learning With Building Foundational Skills and Understandings?

103

INSTRUCTION

HOW DO I USE ASSESSMENT FOR STUDENTS' BENEFIT?

At the beginning of any yoga class, my favorite instructors provide time for people to check in with their bodies and notice how things feel. It's a time for a quick assessment of where I'm tight, what hurts, what my focus might need to be, and I appreciate the reminder, as well as the time. My evaluation and assessment lead to more effective practice, as well as an increased awareness of what I do between yoga classes that could be leading to how I'm feeling.

Just as there are stories that may lead to sore muscles and tight joints, there are stories behind educational data. "What's the story behind the data?" our superintendent asked regularly at Board of Education meetings. As a board member, I used to get reports that indicated how the district was doing as a whole. "Drill down" became a favorite term, as we'd analyze the district's performance, and then a school's, and then sometimes a subgroup or a classroom.

But the more impactful work of assessment was never done at that board table. Instead, that work was done through the daily work of teachers who watched and listened to the students in their classroom every day, reflecting on the learning that was happening and adjusting because of it. As you think about assessment, consider the reasons for it. Some assessments are for accountability, like the ones that we discussed at the Board of Education table, but others are for teaching and learning, for establishing what students have learned and what they should learn next.

This chapter addresses the following questions:

- [ ] **What is assessment?**
- [ ] **What are the types of assessments and their similarities and differences?**
- [ ] **What are some opportunities for assessment, both within instruction and also during practice/independent writing time?**
- [ ] **How do I assess student writing?**
- [ ] **How do I use assessment to provide meaningful feedback to students?**
- [ ] **How do these assessment practices translate when I need to give students a grade or score?**
- [ ] **How do I make sure what I am teaching is clear to students so they will be able to practice a new skill independently?**
- [ ] **How are conferences and small group work opportunities for formative assessment?**
- [ ] **How do I move on if students aren't showing mastery of what I've taught them?**

As you read, think about what you know about students and their writing, how you can find out more, and what you can do with that information. Think about the differences between and the opportunities for both formative and summative assessment, and how any sort of assessment leads to better instruction, and consequently, positive impacts on student learning.

What Is Assessment?

Before we even differentiate between formative and summative assessment, it's important to know that the word *assessment* derives from the Latin root *assidere*, which means to sit beside. When thinking about assessment as a more reflective process, I encourage you to think of assessment more as describing, collecting, and interpreting information about individual students rather than scoring and ranking.

Think about assessment as a process that provides you with information that helps you design lessons and instruct students to raise the level of their learning. Your assessment practices should help you see the evidence of your instruction. If you see minimal evidence, then consider these questions:

- Do I change what I'm teaching?
- Do I change how I'm teaching?
- Do I change what I'm measuring?
- Do I change how I'm measuring?

These questions reflect the relationships between curriculum, instruction, and assessment. As a writing teacher, you need to be clear about what you are teaching students. What do you want them to know and be able to do as writers? Chapter 3 spotlights the instructional moves you'll use to get them there, but throughout all that curriculum and instruction, you need to be a learning detective, constantly evaluating the learning that's happening, the obstacles, and the adjustments you can make to clear the way for students' writing to improve.

As you consider the concepts in this chapter, think about the assessments that *you* have control over. There are some assessments that schools are required to give, generally because of federal or state mandates; you don't decide on the questions, and often you don't see the results or responses in time to make any meaningful adjustments. However, there are many opportunities—even daily opportunities—for you to assess the learning that is happening, and with the knowledge gained from that assessment, you can respond in ways that lead to higher and higher rates of learning and achievement.

Keep in Mind

Developing a repertoire of assessment practices is worth doing since the more efficiently and effectively you assess, the more you can respond, adjust, and impact the learning and achievement in your classroom.

What Are the Types of Assessments and Their Similarities and Differences?

Educators categorize assessment as formative and summative, although overlaps exist between the two. One way to consider the differences between formative and summative assessment is to think about purpose. One reason for assessment is accountability. Stakeholders need to know the patterns and trends of students over time, and results may impact programming and funding. These are often state assessments, mentioned in the previous section, with the results that teachers don't see until students have moved on.

However, assessments also can be used for seeing what has been learned and for making decisions about what to teach next.

When you know and consider the reasons for assessment, you can then categorize, differentiate, and appreciate summative and formative ones.

SUMMATIVE ASSESSMENT

Summative methods are used to collect information about students' progress toward acquiring specific skills and behaviors, assessing students' performance when it comes to achievement and standards. Summative assessment typically happens following instruction. This kind of information informs how effective instruction was for the class and individual students. Considering students' mastery *of* learning, summative assessment might be an on-demand piece of writing at the end of a unit or a performance task to determine students' mastery of learning.

FORMATIVE ASSESSMENT

Formative assessment methods, in turn, are used to identify gaps and plan instruction based on students' progress toward specific goals, providing opportunities for students to learn and practice. When educators are using data to make decisions about what to teach next or to determine what students have learned, they are generally engaged in formative assessments. While you might think of summative assessments as determinations *of* student learning, you can think of formative assessments as *for* student learning.

A formative assessment "is a process used by teachers and students during instruction that provides feedback to adjust ongoing teaching and learning to improve students' achievement of intended instructional outcomes" (Popham, 2011). Formative data collection happens throughout a writing unit, allowing for responsive decisions for instruction. Trumbull and Lash (2013) explain formative assessment as any instructional activity that uncovers how students think about what is being taught and improves their learning.

What Are the Types of Assessments and Their Similarities and Differences?

107

Formative Data Collection	Summative Data Collection
Helps answer the questions: *How can students learn more effectively?* *What are some learning gaps that suggest explicit instruction?* *What might students be ready to learn next?*	Helps answer the question: *Was instruction effective?*
Typically unscored	Typically scored, using a points system, rubric, or progression chart
Takes place *during* instruction, often more than once during a unit	Takes place *after* instruction, usually at the end of a unit or course of study
Used by both teachers *and* students to make adjustments in the learning process	Used mostly by teachers and/or administrators to assess overall learning that happened

THE OVERLAP BETWEEN FORMATIVE AND SUMMATIVE ASSESSMENTS

Both summative and formative assessments serve important purposes within teaching, and the lines between them are not always clear and distinct.

A common metaphor relates them to a chef in the kitchen. As a chef prepares a dish, it's tasted and adjusted throughout the process. The chef's tasting is formative assessment. Customers provide summative assessment since they receive the final product.

However, even in this case, the lines blur. What if a customer provides feedback and suggestions the chef likes? In that case, there could be a return to process through the feedback loop that's the hallmark of formative assessment.

Hopefully, you will see the results of your instruction in this assessment. You might use or create a rubric that scores the writing across traits, or for the categories of structure, development, and conventions. In either case, writing pieces should have clear beginnings, middles, and ends and development that gets stronger as students progress through the grades.

If you are focusing on traits of writing, then you will want to use a rubric that scores ideas, organization, sentence fluency, word choice, conventions, voice, and overall presentation. You may also create or use rubrics for structure, development, and conventions. In either case, you'll want to take time with your district or state's standards to establish what you expect within each category for each grade.

While the differences between formative and summative assessments may blur, it's important to center the reasons for any assessment you're administering. *Why are you assessing?* and *What will you do with the results?* are important questions to know and answer regardless of the process or product.

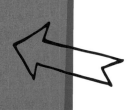

As you develop your understanding of the traits of writing, as well as the structure of your writing classroom, you have many opportunities for assessment, both during instruction and also during independent writing, as well as any time you ask students to write something. During the 2020–2021 school year, when some classes were virtual, a teacher and I had an in-depth conversation about when to assess. Our conversation concluded with the agreement that regardless of platform, we need to be assessing all the time. The chart below lists many of the opportunities for assessment you have during a writing block and throughout a unit.

Formative Data Collection	Summative Data Collection
Pre-assessments	On-demand writing pieces
Observations	Student work in writing folders
Questionnaires	Presentations such as:
Checklists	• Speeches
Discussions	• Oral reports
Conferences	• Readings
Turn and talks	Performance tasks
Notebook entries	
Reflections	
Exit slips	

One way to consider the opportunities for assessment during your writing class is to differentiate between when you're providing direct instruction and when students are engaging in independent writing.

ASSESSMENT DURING INSTRUCTION

As you teach, you can develop the habit of kidwatching, which involves observing children as they take in knowledge (Goodman, 1985). Kidwatching involves studying students' behaviors and processes within a learning environment, and you can do this as you teach. Some questions to guide your kidwatching include:

- Are students paying attention to you?
- If you ask a question, are they able to answer it?
- If you have built in short intervals for students to try out a concept through a conversation or a quick jot, is there evidence that learning is happening?
- How well are students meeting the expectations of their roles during instruction? (Chapter 3 digs into the roles students have during various parts of writing class.)

ASSESSMENT

Keep in Mind

Many teachers use turn and talks during a lesson, but the conversations that happen are shallow at best and do not reflect clear understanding. When providing an opportunity for a turn and talk, make sure there's enough for students to talk about by providing an open-ended question or a challenge of how they'll try the skill in their own writing. Additionally, consider giving a few seconds for thought-gathering before students begin talking.

ASSESSMENT DURING INDEPENDENT WRITING TIME

Chapter 3 emphasizes the importance of independent writing time. During that time, you have opportunities for differentiated instruction, and you also have time to do more kidwatching. You may form small groups based on reading student work, and you can also form small groups based on observations and assessments that you make as you study student work and behaviors during this critical time of writing class. You can circulate and monitor, taking notes and keeping data on behaviors and skills you are seeing.

How do you fit it all in? A structure of independent writing time may look like this:

3–5 minutes	Circulate, monitor, and assess. Have a list of behaviors and skills you are looking for and a system for coding them.
5 minutes	Engage in a conference with a student.
2 minutes	Circulate, monitor, and assess.
5–7 minutes	Small group with four students.
2 minutes	Circulate, monitor, and assess.

Jennifer Serravallo (2010) introduced the concept of engagement inventories, a powerful system of paying attention, monitoring, and fostering the behaviors that lead to higher levels of learning. Serravallo sets up inventories with times across the top, creating sets of data about what students are doing across time intervals. Figure 4.1 shows an example of this concept applied to writing engagement. (You can find a link to a downloadable writing inventory checklist on the online companion, resources.corwin.com/answerselementarywriting.)

Figure 4.1 A writing engagement inventory provides insights into students' writing tendencies.

Writing Engagement Inventory

Date: 11/2/21

Students	Gets started on writing	Has materials ready and organized	Stays on task for more than 10 minutes	Uses tool or resources to be independent
Kate	< 1 minute	3	+	n/a
Ethan	~5	2	2 reminders	n/a
Eli	< 1	4	+	+
Rachel	< 1	4	+	+
Naomi	< 2	3	conf.	+
Mateus	< 2	3	conf.	+
Brooks	< 1	5	+	–
Bruno	*reminders	2	√-	–
Arthur	~5	1	+	n/a
Sally	*reminders	2	√-	+
Ava	left	n/a	n/a	n/a
Nate	< 1	5	+	+
Timmy	< 1	5	+	+

Scale: 1-5
no → yes!
+ - yes!
– - asked me for help

You can also list your students down the left-hand column and the writing behaviors you hope to see across the top. Develop a system for coding your observations, establish a routine for creating a data trail, and you will develop important knowledge and understanding about how students engage in their work. A possible inventory could look like this, but you can customize it for whatever and whoever needs attention.

Regardless of how you set up your tracking system, you want to be clear about what you are assessing and how you will collect data that gives you useful information for both teaching and learning.

How Do I Assess Student Writing?

Many teachers feel pressure to pore through and analyze student writing, and yes, it's possible to learn a lot about students as writers through those sorts of close reads. However, as you develop, you become clearer and clearer about what you are looking for, and you will be able to make instructional decisions more quickly.

READ AND DISCUSS WITH SPECIFIC LENSES

It's possible to read over students' shoulders, take a few notes, and make some instructional decisions, especially if you are looking for specific qualities and prioritizing consistent components. When I read a student's piece, I may look for volume and comfort with getting ideas onto a page. If I don't see that happening, I may engage in a conversation with the student about what's getting in the way. Maybe it's a lack of idea, but maybe it has more to do with spelling, neatness, or even physical discomfort while writing. From there, I try to establish that the writer has a plan that establishes structure for the piece. If the writer is working on a narrative piece, I tend to ask about the beginning, middle, and end. With information pieces, I want to know what topics the readers will be learning. When a writer is working on an opinion piece, I look for evidence of a clear claim and reasons or ideas that address the claim.

Once I see structure, I look for evidence of development that relates closely to volume and productivity. Many teachers prioritize conventions and spelling more than I do, although those elements of writing matter to me. However, I assess first for ideas and understanding of purpose before I analyze spelling, sentence structure, and conventions.

DEVELOP YOUR PRACTICE OF SORTING STUDENT WORK

Every now and then—and it varies depending on ages and stages of writers—you might consider collecting work in progress or recently finished pieces and doing some quick sorts, a process that takes much less time than close reads and analysis. When doing a quick sort, list out some look-fors that relate closely to what you've been teaching in class. For example, if you are teaching a narrative writing unit, you might sort pieces into piles based on which pieces:

- Have a clear beginning, middle, and end
- Use dialogue effectively
- Hook the reader with a catchy lead
- Are ready for paragraphs

Customize lists like this based on the students in your class and the lessons you've been giving, sort their daily work, and you've used assessment to determine small groups of responsive teaching points!

Keep in Mind

It's easier to read the entire pieces of most younger students' writing than it is to read the entire pieces of many older students. As students move through the grades, their pieces should get longer and more complex. If you are working with older students, you can sort pieces based on specific features without reading the entire text.

PRIORITIZE PRE-ASSESSMENTS

In addition to the daily observations, conferences, checklists, and self-assessments, you have assessment opportunities at the beginning and end of a unit. A **pre-assessment** asks students to show what they know about the upcoming lessons and what they can already do. You can say something along the lines of "Today I want you to write a piece that shows me all you already know about information writing." Depending on the grade, you can create a chart of what they might include in their writing. You can also create a wall chart of how to do it, like the ones shown in Figures 4.2 and 4.3. These charts will be useful during the pre-assessment and throughout the unit, as well. Think of this as an on-demand piece of writing because you are not giving direct instruction for any component of it. This piece of writing should reflect what students know and are able to do without conferring or specific suggestions.

Figures 4.2 and 4.3 A combination of anchor and process charts can be introduced to mid-upper elementary students before giving a pre- or post-assessment as reminders for what they should be doing in a narrative story.

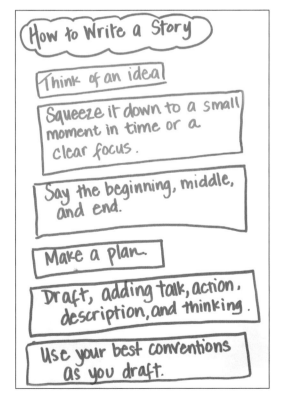

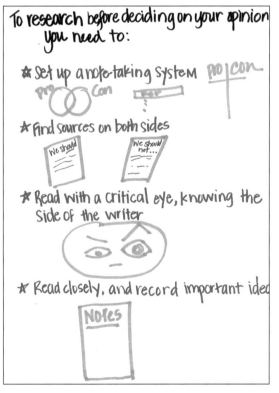

Source: Meehan (2019).

ASSESSMENT

On-demand assessments, whether at the beginning or end of a unit, offer the chance to see what students are able to do on their own. These assessments will answer: If you or another adult are not making constant suggestions or offering continuous prompts, then what can a student write on their own? How much can students produce? How long can they sustain attention and engagement to their piece of work? Assessing on-demand writing can provide you with invaluable information about how students are internalizing and transferring skills and knowledge about writing.

Keep in Mind

Pre-assessments do not require rigid procedures and protocols. Walk around as students are writing a pre-assessment piece and give plenty of specific comments and compliments. Pay attention to who can hear your comments and make changes right then and there. How students respond to feedback is important information to gather whenever you can.

On-Demand Writing Piece	Process Writing Piece
• Written by student without teacher direction • Typically happens at the beginning and end of a writing unit • Used to determine what a student knows, next steps for teaching, and what they've learned • Written during the span of one to three class periods	• Student incorporates suggestions and feedback from teacher or peers • Used to guide instructional decisions • Written over a longer period of time than an on-demand • Longer periods of time vary depending on the age and level of writers; students with more experience and confidence can spend longer amounts of time on process pieces

At the end of a writing unit, you'll want to ask students to write another on-demand writing piece, this time showing all they've learned.

Equity and Access

Pay attention to whether students become *stuck* at any given point during the writing process. If they do, then consider bridging the gap for them but making note of a skill that still needs work.

Students' process pieces often are much stronger than their on-demand pieces. This pattern in your classroom may suggest that there may be too much input into the process pieces. Students need to practice and internalize skills to retain them. If the instructional balance leans too much toward step-by-step instruction or directives, retention and transfer may not happen.

How Do I Use Assessment to Provide Meaningful Feedback to Students?

At any point in writing instruction, feedback is a critical element to keep in mind. You can offer students feedback both in terms of what they *are* doing and what they are *not* doing. The more you notice and comment on what they are doing, the greater likelihood that it will continue, so if student writing is showing evidence of instruction and learning, you definitely want to point it out. When I am offering feedback to students, I always try to balance the positives with the next steps because I want students to approach writing with a confident mindset.

DEVELOP AND MAINTAIN AN ASSET-BASED APPROACH

Most of the time, when you read student writing, you are assessing it. There may be a few times when you read a student piece of writing for entertainment, to learn something, or to challenge or affirm your opinion, but most of the time you are reading and considering how the student did any one of those things. One read, especially for some pieces, may be to understand the words and sentences. Sometimes, spelling and syntax need some deciphering. But at that point, consider the question of *what is this writer doing effectively?* as opposed to *what do I need to teach or develop in this writer?* What writers are doing well matters and counts as data. You can create a chart like the one below to nurture your asset-based approach.

Student	What are they doing well?	What could next steps be?

When assessment is seen as a time to *sit beside*, opportunities exist throughout writing instruction, regardless of program or instructional model. This way of thinking about assessment also helps keep the approach positive for both teachers and students.

CREATE SYSTEMS FOR KEEPING TRACK OF ASSESSMENT

Because writing is complex, integrating skills and behaviors, it helps to categorize those skills and behaviors and create systems and structures for observing and assessing them.

As you categorize and think about systems, you'll want to think about and include behaviors, as well as skills. What are the behaviors you expect from students? Some behaviors might include, but aren't limited to,

Keep in Mind

Before you read student writing to decide on a teaching point, read to connect personally or emotionally to what that student has written. There is great value in getting to know your students and building relationships this way!

ASSESSMENT

Keep in Mind

You do not have to fill every moment of independent writing time with verbal interactions between you and students. Allow yourself time to circulate and assess students as they are independently writing. Resist the urge to jump from one conference to another without taking the time to watch and notice what students are doing.

- Gather all necessary materials for a productive writing period
- Establish a place and a routine that leads to getting started within a minute or so
- Read and reread pieces to know what to work on next
- Ask for conferences or direct instruction when needed
- Express goals and priorities for their own writing work

Once you establish this list of expectations for student writing, then you can set up your system for collecting evidence. Depending on your level of comfort with digital platforms, you could use Google Forms or a pen-and-paper system. The Learning Target Collecting sheet shown in Figure 4.4 is available for download from the companion website, resources.corwin.com/answerselementarywriting.

Taking the time to customize and use a sheet like this is worth it because it helps you assess and monitor your teaching and the evidence of learning. As you use any data collection system, make sure to establish a code for yourself so that you know that the skill is mastered, developing, emerging, or not showing up at all yet.

What really matters is that you have a system that works for you, you follow it, and both you and your students know and understand their progress and next steps. That is assessment at work for evaluating student learning, providing meaningful feedback, and deciding on next instructional steps.

Figure 4.4 This collection sheet is set up for a third-grade narrative writing unit. Students' names are written down in the first column, and the set of skills and traits are across the top. Keeping this close at hand allows for quick record-keeping as you circulate the room.

Collecting Evidence

Students	Learning Targets—I can:											
Names	Identify the structure of writing workshop– both my role and my teacher's role.	Gather supplies that help me be a good writer.	Find ideas from my own life that are story-worthy.	Plan stories with a beginning, middle, and end.	Use a checklist to self-assess and set goals as a writer	Use everything I know about spelling to be independent as I write.	Use specific strategies to bring my story to life	Use all I know about conventions as I write.	Use the craft moves I notice in books in my own writing.	Use paragraphs correctly as I draft.	Maintain writing stamina.	Initiate a writing task.

CREATE VISUALS FOR STUDENTS WHENEVER POSSIBLE

You might consider developing feedback forms that you share with students. As with conferring cards (see Chapter 3), feedback forms give students the visual representation of what they're doing well, with a nudge toward important skills they need to keep practicing. A sample feedback form could look like Figure 4.5.

Because I am always working toward having students take over ownership of their writing and learning lives, you'll notice on this feedback form, I have purposely left a blank line so that the student may also contribute a next step.

Figure 4.5 Feedback forms provide clarity for students of both strengths and possible next steps.

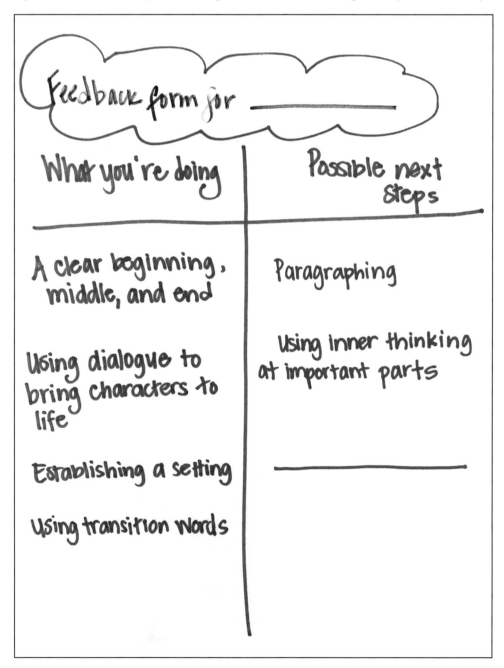

How Do I Use Assessment to Provide Meaningful Feedback to Students?

117

ASSESSMENT

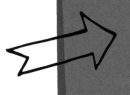

How Do These Assessment Practices Translate When I Need to Give Students a Grade or Score?

On-demand writing assessments are important because they provide information for you to see what students are able to do independently within a set amount of time. As students write those pieces, you have the opportunity to watch them through various lenses.

KNOW WHAT YOU ARE LOOKING FOR

Grading differs from district to district, and you will want to know what you should specifically be evaluating. For example, you may be evaluating students' ability to:

- Think of ideas for writing
- Initiate and sustain a writing task
- Apply revision and editing skills

You may also be grading specific features or traits of the writing piece. Chapter 2 addresses the traits of effective writing, and knowing the grade-level characteristics of those traits will help you grade or score student writing. It is rare for a single piece of writing to have the same score across all traits. A piece may exceed standards for organization but approach standards for conventions. Another piece may meet standards for ideas and organization but approach when it comes to development or elaboration.

CONSIDER DEVELOPING A CUMULATIVE OR COMPOSITE SCORING SYSTEM

One way to make it easier to spot patterns and trends is to create systems that total students' overall scores by adding up single scores on traits. For example, you might decide that scores align as follows:

- Below grade-level standards: 1
- Approaching grade-level standards: 2
- Meeting grade-level standards: 3
- Exceeding grade-level standards: 4

If you develop a scoring system across six traits, then the highest score a student could get would be a 24, and the lowest would be a 6. Although a student may not get an 18 with six 3s, you could think of an 18 as about what you'd expect for the grade-level standard.

Overall, how you grade students should align with your district's practices. Some districts are standards-based, while others grade numerically or with letters. Whatever you decide, you'll want to be clear with students, families, and yourself about how and why the grade is what it is. The clearer the criteria, the clearer the pathway toward growth and achievement.

How Do I Make Sure What I Am Teaching Is Clear to Students So They Will Be Able to Practice a New Skill Independently?

As you develop your kidwatching lens, you'll get better and better at looking for the evidence of instruction in student work. One question I ask students is, "Where is the evidence of my great instruction?" They look at me and sometimes giggle, but this question is an important one to answer, for both teachers and students.

ESTABLISH CLARITY OF YOUR TEACHING OBJECTIVE

One way to assess clarity is to make sure that you can state the skill you expect to see. Chapter 3 discusses the importance of a clear teaching point. Are you able to state what it is that you are teaching and looking for from students' writing? If you can, then the probability increases of students being able to state the learning goals, too.

Once you establish that both you and students know what you're teaching, you can have more effective conversations and reflections about where there is evidence of instruction. You can also have better information about what next steps should be. If students understand the concept but haven't been able to implement it, then they may need more practice. If they don't understand the concept, then they may need additional instruction or they may not be ready for it.

Remember the purposes of assessment. You are constantly evaluating what students know and understand and what next instructional steps make the most sense along their learning pathway.

INVITE STUDENT INPUT AND EXPLANATION

After you teach a concept, you can develop the practice of asking students to explain, in their words, what you taught. This practice will help you clarify whatever you are teaching as you listen to the various interpretations. Additionally, this practice builds speaking and listening skills of students.

At the end of a whole group lesson, you can ask for a student to explain what you taught. Invite others to add on or explain it in a different way. Likewise, you can close out an individual conference or a small group session by asking students what they learned and what they will be practicing as a result of the instruction. Sometimes I ask students to create a visual for themselves on the back of one of the pink conference cards (see Chapter 3) to help them remember. "I can tell you what I taught in my words," I will say to students, "but it's more important for you to be able to say it in *your* words." Once students know this question is coming, they are apt to pay more attention to your teaching as well.

In *Classroom Instruction That Works* (Marzano et al., 2004), one of the high-impact instructional strategies involves note-taking and summarizing. This practice leans into the power of summarizing, and it also communicates to you whether students have clarity before they head off to independent writing time.

Agency and Identity

Remember the conference cards in Chapter 3? Those conference cards are not only an important instructional tool, but they are also an assessment tool because if you ask students to tell you what to write for the learning point, then you are assessing their understanding of what the expectation was for their learning. If they can't say what they learned, then they probably can't show the evidence of it in their writing either!

PROVIDE TIMELY AND DIRECT FEEDBACK

You've provided clarity with an established learning objective, you've captured student input by asking for their explanation or summary of the learning, and now students are off to work on their writing independently. Independent writing time is the time when they'll be practicing the skill, so you don't want them to forget their intention! This is when you can use feedback to maintain that intention.

The following phrases are great starters to keep close at hand as you circulate and read students' writing, using your teaching point to fill in the blank:

- I notice that you have _____
- You are starting to _____
- I see the evidence of _____

Remember that even snippets of feedback are powerful for blending assessment with intentional practice. When other students in the vicinity hear these sorts of comments, it could also help them remember the learning objective and focus their practice.

Notes

Answers to Your Biggest Questions About Teaching Elementary Writing

How Are Conferences and Small Group Work Opportunities for Formative Assessment?

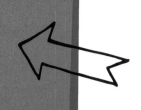

In a highly functional writing classroom, students can communicate what they are working on with their teacher and with each other. Remember that the goal is to teach the writer and not the writing, so it's important that whatever students are working on involves skills and knowledge that will benefit subsequent pieces and not just the current one.

MAKE SURE STUDENTS TAKE AN ACTIVE ROLE DURING DIFFERENTIATED INSTRUCTION

Small group and individual instruction, as noted in Chapter 3, are powerful formats for targeting skills and differentiated instruction. Small group work and conferring with students are instructional practices, and they are also opportunities for formative assessment. During conferences, you can glean the following assessment data:

- Can students explain what they are working on? How do they do that?
- Do they have a goal that they are working on?
- Is that goal transferable or only relevant for that particular piece?
- What are the students' challenges?
- Are they showing mastery of any skills? How can you leverage those skills to help them grow others?

Regardless of how you begin your differentiated instruction, students should know that you expect their participation. They should have a goal they are working on and be able to state it.

The conference cards that are described in Chapter 3 summarize the compliment and the teaching point, and they also have space to write in a challenge. That challenge serves as priorities and next steps. The more students are able to describe and understand every part of the conference card, the more they are able to develop agency—setting goals, creating a plan, and getting to work on achieving them.

CREATE SYSTEMS AND STRUCTURES FOR STUDENTS TO COMMUNICATE WHAT THEY ARE WORKING ON

You can assess what students are working on by circulating and kidwatching in your writing classrooms, and you can also involve students in communicating what they are working on, whether they feel the need for a conference, and what the focus of the conference should be.

Another system for involving students in communicating their priorities and next steps is to create seminar sign-ups, such as those described in Chapter 5. The more students know and understand what they need to work on next, the more effectively

Keep in Mind

It doesn't have to be the teacher's job to fill out the conference cards. By asking students to fill out their own cards, you are shifting agency. What students write should be indicative of what they understand. Use this information to adjust and inform your instruction.

ASSESSMENT

How Are Conferences and Small Group Work Opportunities for Formative Assessment?

121

you can teach and they can learn. When students know what they are working on, that indicates their agency and understanding of their own process and progression.

A Google Form is another system for establishing communication. Just a few questions provide a significant amount of information:

- Name
- Current writing goal
    - Short answer
- Conference?
    - Yes
    - No

Figure 4.6 is an example of a form showing the types of questions you might ask. You can establish how often students fill it out, but when students know and expect these questions, they work with more direction and purpose. (Find a link to this Google Form on the online companion website, resources.corwin.com/answerselementarywriting.)

Figure 4.6 Using a Google Form leads to the population of a spreadsheet and provides information about students' progress as writers.

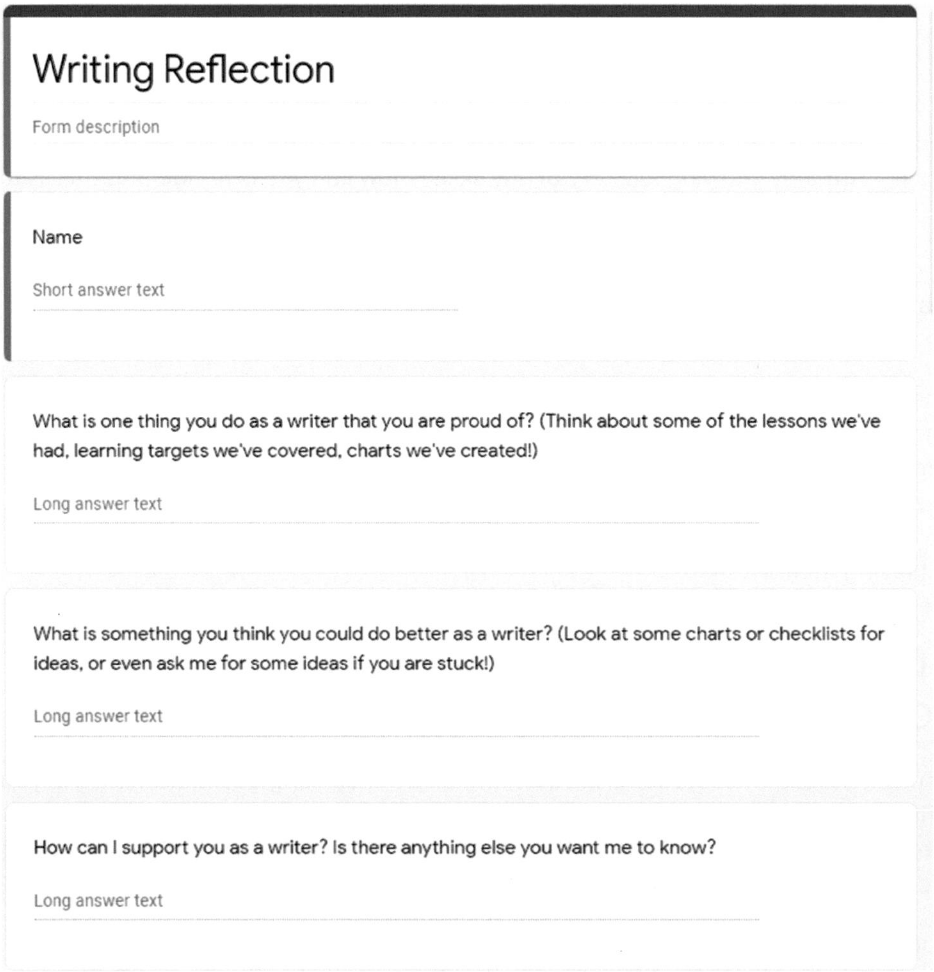

Writing Reflection

Form description

Name

Short answer text

What is one thing you do as a writer that you are proud of? (Think about some of the lessons we've had, learning targets we've covered, charts we've created!)

Long answer text

What is something you think you could do better as a writer? (Look at some charts or checklists for ideas, or even ask me for some ideas if you are stuck!)

Long answer text

How can I support you as a writer? Is there anything else you want me to know?

Long answer text

KNOW NEXT STEPS AND PRIORITIES

The clarity of your instruction directly relates to how well students understand next steps and priorities. Do they know success criteria for whatever they are working on? You can establish this understanding by creating access to learning tools such as anchor charts and learning progressions. The more students know what they are aiming for, the more effectively they can work toward success!

In a February 2018 ASCD article, Doug Fisher and Nancy Frey explain learning targets and success criteria by using a GPS analogy. The destination is analogous to the learning target. Do you know where you're heading, and can you get there? The success criteria relate to the various turns you take along the way to your destination. Do the moves you make and the learning that happens result in moving you toward your ultimate destination?

Knowing and being clear about learning targets and the success criteria associated with them helps students with their intentional practice.

Terms to Know

Success Criteria: progress toward a destination.

Learning Target: this is what you want students to know and be able to do by the end of one or more lessons.

ADJUST ACCORDINGLY

Even when you know the destination, if we continue the driving analogy, there may be times that the hills are too steep or there are roadblocks in the way. Therefore adjustments become necessary, but you have to make those adjustments based on the assessment of where you are at that point in time. In teaching and learning, it could be that these adjustments involve a change in expectation, even though the learning target may be the same, and that change in expectation should be based on the assessment of current skills and understanding.

Therefore, it's important to develop your ability to think in terms of learning progressions, thinking about the skills and understandings that have to be in place before others can happen. Remember the group of adults who were trying (or not trying) to place their palms on the floor? To get to that place of flexibility, they had to assess their starting point, and then work toward a different level of flexibility first.

How Do I Move On if Students Aren't Showing Mastery of What I've Taught Them?

There are times when you will reach a point in a writing unit where students are mostly done with their growth. They've thought of all the stories they know, they've tried a variety of strategies, and they've revised and edited to the point where they no longer spot mistakes or recognize issues. Sometimes, the wisest decision you can make is to move on, even if not everyone has shown mastery of all learning targets or has learned as much as you think they should. When this is the case, what can you do?

CELEBRATE GROWTH OVER MASTERY

Almost any athletic endeavor involves the integration of many skills to be successful, and the more those skills come together, the more success an athlete might experience. As someone learns to swim the crawl stroke, for instance, kicking is important. Legs should stay straight. Arm strokes also matter, and fingers should be cupped, not spread. And then breathing has to happen with the head moving to the side in time with the arm stroke. For a new swimmer to make it across the pool, every part of the stroke does not have to be in place, but a solid approximation should be happening.

This analogy works for writing, as well. Success in writing involves the integration of many skills, and as one develops or the focus and energy are on it, another skill might slack or falter. Approximation is a helpful framework for thinking about the process with a general and overall growth progression that may not always follow the same slope. Sometimes instruction involves reminders. *Don't forget to use all you know about capitalization; good introductions have hooks, so make sure yours does; transition words help with the flow of your writing* . . . These sorts of statements serve a similar purpose as the statements and reminders a swim instructor makes as their swimmers work at making it the length of the pool.

As you consider moving on without mastery from all students, keep in mind the importance of not letting perfect get in the way of the good. Writers are on a constant quest, and there is always revision to be made. If you think about *growth* as opposed to mastery, you might feel more comfortable with moving on.

It's also helpful to remember that not every piece is for publication. Some pieces are for practice. Maybe a writer works on structure with intention on one piece. Maybe the focus of another piece is on using more precise language. And maybe there's a piece where the writer is working hard at considering the audience and making sure that readers will envision or understand the intent of the piece.

When you have collected data throughout a unit, you have a record of what students know and are able to do. With this information, you can cycle back to skills through other content areas. Writing does not happen in isolation; there are opportunities—requirements, even—to write in other content areas where the instruction and learning focus might be science, math, social studies, or another subject. You can cue students to work on specific skills within the domain of writing as they are learning and expressing their knowledge about other topics.

PROVIDE ADDITIONAL OPPORTUNITIES FOR WRITING IN OTHER CONTENT AREAS

When you establish clarity of expectations for students, provide instruction for those expectations, and communicate progress, then you should expect skills to show up in other places. Writing is not a skill that happens in isolation, and the more you weave in writing opportunities throughout content areas, the more transfer is likely to happen. But hold students' feet to the fire when it comes to using what they know! If they've learned how to use paragraphs, then remind them to use paragraphs in their science explanation. If clear sentencing was a goal, then it's still a goal as they communicate their mathematical thinking. Even when students didn't master learning targets during the writing unit, you can still provide practice opportunities in other areas.

End-of-Chapter Reflections

What might you try when it comes to assessment within the next week? The next month?

As you consider your assessment strategies, what elements feel strong and secure? What are some elements that you consider opportunities for growth?

What are three goals that you are setting related to assessment?

chapter FIVE

HOW DO I SHIFT AGENCY FROM TEACHER TO STUDENTS IN THE WRITING CLASSROOM?

A friend who has been a camp counselor for many years loves to talk about the first couple of days with campers who are experiencing their first away-from-home adventure. Many first-time campers need explicit instruction about putting away their things, taking care of themselves, and being respectful of others. He looks forward to when those routines are all in place, kids are doing things on their own, and his job is simply to remind campers when necessary.

As you read this chapter, think about how to engage students in taking ownership of their own learning, collaborative work, discussion, vocabulary development, and other ideas related to communicating about writing. Throughout this book, there have been many mentions of student agency, but this chapter addresses it directly, offering ways to increase how students build their own understanding of themselves within their writing lives.

I encourage you to think about what independence means to you when it comes to the writers in your classroom. How do you assess independence, and what structures and systems support its development? How do you determine that what you're teaching is what students are practicing and learning? Thinking about these questions helps build a writing community where students begin to take charge of their own writing lives, developing agency and purpose as communicators in their world.

This chapter takes on the questions:

- [ ] **What is agency in a writing classroom?**
- [ ] **How can the environment support independence and agency?**
- [ ] **How can I nurture partnerships and productive conversations between students?**
- [ ] **How do I support student thinking and discussion without taking over?**
- [ ] **How do I engage students in self-assessment?**
- [ ] **How can I encourage students to set goals and decide on next steps?**

Just as those campers need instructions, directions, and checklists for specific activities and parts of the days, writers need them for specific parts of writing instruction, and it's a worthy time investment to establish the mindsets of lifelong writers.

What Is Agency in a Writing Classroom?

When Kelsey Sorum and I (2021) were writing *The Responsive Writing Teacher*, we had several discussions about what it meant to be responsible for learning. Whose responsibility was it that students developed as writers? Ultimately, we agreed that the responsibility for learning lay on the shoulders of the teachers. That being said, the more we could shift agency from teacher to student, the more possibility for high rates of learning. By agency, we envision how well students understand what they are learning, what they might learn next, and how much it matters to them that they do that learning.

As you consider the various components of your writing instruction, you might ask yourself some of these questions to understand student agency. Do students:

- Know each other as people and as writers?
- Make decisions about what pieces to share and initiate sharing them?
- Use the systems and structures within the classroom to work independently and take on challenges when they happen?
- Understand ways and questions to support each other as writers, regardless of where other people are in their process?
- Have resources to use to evaluate success?
- Self-assess and set goals?

When I enter a writing classroom, I look for evidence of what learning has been happening, both to ground myself and to see how well students are likely to know. Can I look around and determine what has been taught and emphasized recently? If I can, then chances are that students can also, and if they can, then they have resources to help them learn and grow as writers even when the teacher is not available.

As you develop an environment where you can answer many of the questions above affirmatively, then students are developing agency. When students have agency for their learning, they are on a pathway toward becoming authentic writers who understand, appreciate, and initiate the power of writing.

How Can the Environment Support Independence and Agency?

Chapter 1 discusses many of the systems and structures you can build and establish to create routine and predictability. As you think about the roles students play during any type of instruction, you'll want to consider how actively students are taking on their roles. Student choice is critical for independence and agency, and the amount of initiative and innovation you can create in the classroom also leads to independence and agency.

ENHANCE THE OPPORTUNITIES FOR STUDENT CHOICE THROUGHOUT WRITING INSTRUCTION

"What will they be writing about?" a parent asked before the start of an online writing summer class I offered. She was a former teacher, and I knew that her question really involved whether I'd be assigning topics or figuring out what mattered to students and getting them to write from those topics. (I was!) Offering choice to writers and inspiring them to write about what matters to them is one of my core beliefs about powerful writing instruction, and choice of writing topic builds agency for writers without a doubt. Whenever you can, you will want to offer writers their choice of topics, whether those topics are ones of passion and knowledge for them or ones of curiosity and wonder.

There will be times when writers must write about a given topic—maybe for a specific assignment or assessment, maybe because they just can't come up with a topic of their own and it has become a chronic source of stuckness for them—but there are still ways to infuse choice into writing instruction. Let's think about various elements within writing instruction and possible choices that could exist.

Element of Instruction	Possible Choices
Preparation	• Pens or pencils • Paper or computer • Types of paper
Environment	• Place within the classroom • Alone or with collaborators • Headphones for music or silence
Planning	• Length of time spent on the planning process • Types of planners
Collaboration	• Working with partners or groups • Requesting a conference or seminar • Deciding on goals or next steps

Remember that choice in any of these elements can be seen as a privilege, and making decisions is a skill. Sometimes, writers might make the most progress if you make some choices for them with a plan in place for giving that choice back. You will want to constantly evaluate the choices writers make as you are teaching them so that you can guide them to make the most effective decisions for their own learning and writing lives.

CREATE AND REMIND STUDENTS OF RESOURCES THAT HELP THEM WHEN THEY ARE STUCK

Student agency grows if children can identify resources in the room that help them besides their teacher. Some of the resources may include:

- Classroom charts that describe expectations or processes
- Checklists that contain indicators or expectations for written work
- Mentor texts that inspire and invite students to try new things
- Exemplar texts that have been written by other students, demonstrating what students are aiming for as writers

A quick activity that provides insight into how (and if) students use the resources within their classroom is to ask them to go and stand next to something that they use that helps them learn. Take note of who goes where, and then ask them to go to another resource. You might be surprised by what students value and what they don't! You can even create a chart of what resources are available to students when you're not available. Figure 5.1 shows a possible chart that you could create for or with students, reminding them of all they have to support themselves.

Figure 5.1 A chart of resources available to students provides a visual reminder for them.

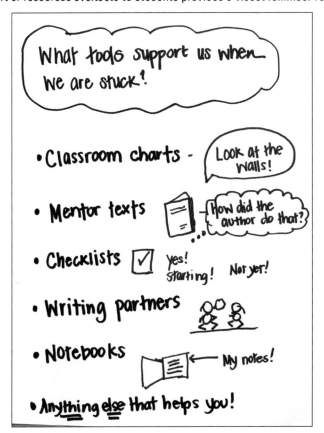

Writers develop agency when they understand their role and they have tools to use for that role. A chart like Figure 5.1 does not need to be writing specific. This chart could include other resources and serve as a reminder of resources and expectation for agency in all content areas.

MAKE SURE STUDENTS KNOW WHEN, WHERE, AND HOW TO ACCESS MATERIALS

Even if students have not co-designed materials, they should know when, where, and how to access them. It's worth taking the time to provide instruction on what Meghan Hargrave (2020) calls "the silent teachers" of the room. As your writing classroom develops, you probably have more silent teachers than you realize—and certainly more than your students realize! Charts, checklists, mentor texts, demonstration pieces, conferring cards—those are all silent teachers that, if students are accessing and using, build agency and independence.

Even when you teach students what those silent teachers are, you might still need to teach them *how* to use them. That lesson will depend on how you've set up the resources in your classroom. Here are some suggestions for how to make materials accessible for students:

- Create a bulletin board of writing charts that students can look at
- Provide small versions or digital versions of those charts for students to take to their working space
- Make a shelf of mentor texts or photocopied pages of particularly relevant passages that students know they can access during independent writing time

Students will need some direct instruction and possibly even a protocol for using a silent teacher. For example, Hargrave shares a clear protocol for teaching students to use a checklist. First, students must read part of the checklist, then they should notice and note what that checklist indicator looks like in a piece of writing *other than their own*—a mentor text or a demonstration text. At that point, students can look closely at their own writing, asking themselves if their writing shows that indicator or if they could do it better. For any of the other resources you offer—the silent teachers of your classrooms—you can develop your own systems using Hargrave's as a model.

INVITE STUDENTS INTO THE PROCESS OF CREATING

My oldest daughter, Larkin, loved to create special spaces for herself when she was younger. She shared a room with her sister, but her part of the room was full of her artwork and the special flourishes she could create with any materials she could find and repurpose. Additionally, she loved to have organizational spaces, and she always knew where to find things.

Larkin's spaces created ownership and pride, pillars of agency. Just as she created her spaces within her bedroom, students can participate in planning and creating the elements of their writing classroom. You might start with some of the following ideas:

- Where should we keep the materials that you will use during writing time?
- What materials do you as writers need to have on hand?
- How should we set up specific places throughout the room for your optimal working conditions?

Any of these questions serve as inquiry lessons (see Chapter 3) or invitations to participate in the set-up and maintenance of a productive writing environment. They also help students begin to think of themselves as writers.

While you can promote agency by providing these materials for students, you promote even more agency by having students create their own tools. Many carpenters favor the tools they design themselves because they know exactly how to use them!

If you establish the expectation that as you teach, students create some sort of artifact or visual for themselves to hold on to the new learning, then students could be designing tools for themselves all the time. This could be in their writer's notebook. I've also seen teachers create student toolkits or keyrings that become students' go-to resources that they've created themselves. (The following figures show examples of student-created tools.)

"Make yourself a tool so that you remember what you've learned" is a powerful statement for fostering student agency.

Figure 5.2 A keyring holds personalized charts and resources a student created.

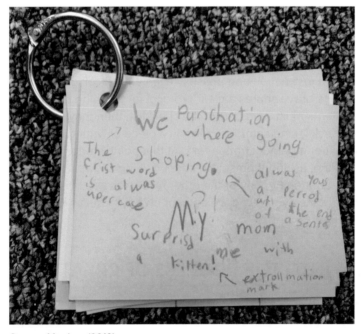

Source: Meehan (2019).

Figure 5.3 Cardstock on hand allows students to design their own learning tools.

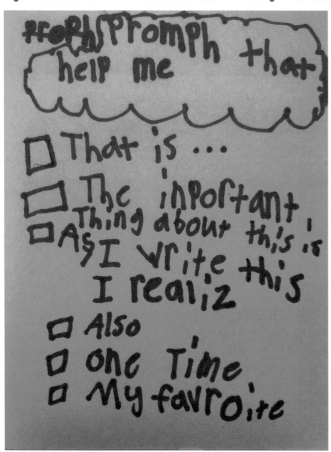

Source: Meehan (2019).

Figure 5.4 A spiral-bound booklet organizes student-made resources.

Source: Meehan & Sorum (2021).

Keep in Mind

The most effective tools are the ones that are used. When students create their own tools, they understand the meaning, the purpose, and the value, and they know and understand how to use them.

How Can I Nurture Partnerships and Productive Conversations Between Students?

When I was working on my MFA in creative writing, there were times when our leader did not say much because the feedback and comments from the members of the group were strong enough. Never did I feel that the leaders weren't in charge, but there were times when I appreciated the wisdom of other students as much as any of the commentary from the leaders. This is the hope for a strong writing class where students feel the same sort of agency that we did as MFA students.

Participation in the learning process is a critical life skill regardless of the content area, and writing instruction is a time and place for developing it.

PROVIDE OPPORTUNITIES FOR PRODUCTIVE CONVERSATIONS

There are times when you will be asking students to have a conversation as a part of your instruction. Many teachers refer to these times as turn and talks. These can be good opportunities for children to learn and reinforce learning, as well as an opportunity for some formative assessment. However, if students are going to benefit or increase the influence they have on each other's learning, there are a few caveats.

First, the question you ask them to discuss must be conversation worthy. If the question can be answered with a single word or just a few words, then it's hard to sustain a conversation regardless of the intention or experience. The table below suggests ways you can revise a question to be conversation worthy.

Thinking About Conversation-Worthy Questions	
Instead of . . .	**Try this . . .**
What kind of lead did the author use?	The author chose a specific type of lead. What is the impact on the readers?
Where are some transitional phrases in this piece of writing?	Where and how do the transitional phrases help readers follow the writer's line of thinking?
Where does the writer use punctuation for impact on the reader?	What are the impacts of the punctuation the writer has chosen to use?

You'll want to teach students how to have a conversation, even from a physical aspect. Depending on the age and experience of the students, you may need to teach them how to turn and face each other, decide who will speak first, look and listen to each other, and react or respond to one another. Speaking and listening are critical communication skills, so these lessons are worth the time!

Many students become masters at saying very little during conversations, and you'll want to intervene and change those patterns. Some ways of doing that include asking students to:

- Share the most important part of their conversation
- Share something important their partner said
- Jot down a few takeaways from the conversation

These moves hold students accountable to themselves, each other, and the larger group for contributing and sharing knowledge, insights, and reflections.

Keep in Mind

Many effective conversationalists require some time to gather their thoughts. When you ask students to have a conversation, give them a few seconds before they begin talking about it. That way, students have a chance to gather their thoughts and most conversations will go better because of that reflection time.

FOSTER MEANINGFUL PARTNERSHIPS

Partnerships have the potential to be powerful learning opportunities for students in writing classrooms, but just as productive conversations require guidance and coaching, so do meaningful partnerships. One of the first things you must establish is the shared language and understanding of the writing process (see Chapter 1). Once everyone understands the basic components of the writing process, then you can teach into what questions correlate to what parts of the process, and they can deepen the power of their questions. This learning can happen intentionally, and you may include it as a lesson with direct instruction or through an inquiry lesson. The chart below shows some partnership questions that correlate with various parts of the writing process.

Part of the Writing Process	Possible Questions That a Partner Could Ask a Writer
Generating	• What are you thinking you might write about? • What have you been really interested in lately? • What do you already know a lot about? • What are some moments that have stood out to you lately—maybe times when you've felt scared, angry, or embarrassed?
Planning	• What sections are you envisioning? • How would you tell the story, thinking about the beginning, middle, and end? • What are the reasons you have for your opinion?
Drafting/Revising	• What are you working on to develop your piece? • Are there areas you want me to focus on to make sure they're clear? • Is there a spot I can help you think or talk through?
Editing	• Are there conventions that get confusing to you? • Do you want me to tell you how I'd read this based on your punctuation?

ENCOURAGE SELF-REFLECTION ON CONVERSATION AND COLLABORATION

As routines start to set in place, you can begin to shift agency by asking students to pay attention to their own level of contribution. This may be a checklist, a Google Form, or any other system of self-assessment that you introduce to the students in your classroom.

It's important to keep track of a few things when it comes to raising voices:

- Do students have something they feel is shareworthy?
- Do they have a response for a question?
- Do students have no idea?
- Are students aware of their silence or their lack thereof?

AGENCY

With these questions in mind, you can create systems for gathering data. The following rating scale is an example of a self-reflection you might ask students to fill out, either on paper or online:

Name:				Date:
Question or situation	4	3	2	1
	I shared, and I think it was the right balance with the amount I listened to and learned from others.	I shared, and it might have been too much compared to how much I listened to and learned from others.	I had something to share, but I did not contribute much to the conversation or lesson.	I didn't have anything to share—not much writing I felt comfortable with or not many responses I felt good about.

This sort of scale lends itself to a fist-to-three method of quick assessment: Ask students to hold up fists for the equivalent of a 1, one finger for a 2, and so on up to three fingers for just the right amount of balanced sharing and listening.

Whatever system you create, the information you collect reveals patterns of collaboration and contribution that you will want to reinforce or develop. Share the data with students and challenge them to work on their contributions, regardless of the pattern or reason.

You'll need to teach and then support these conversational skills. Students don't automatically understand the nuances of contributing, listening, and building on ideas.

Notes

How Do I Support Student Thinking and Discussion Without Taking Over?

In any conversation, there's a temptation to take over and weigh in with your knowledge and insights, but be careful of doing this. You don't want the takeaway to be that students can't engage in important conversations without you! You want to build their ability and agency to initiate and sustain their own thinking and learning, and there are strategies you can use to build that ability.

HAVE STUDENTS TURN AWAY FROM YOU

This is a simple strategy, but one that signals expectation, confidence, and agency of students; I first saw Shana Frazin, a staff developer from Teachers College, use it. After teaching a small group of students, she asked students to discuss their learning and their planned next steps, but she asked students to turn *away from her*. This removed the temptation of them engaging her into the conversation, although she could still listen to what they were saying.

USE "TALKING IN" AS A STRATEGY TO SUPPORT STUDENTS

Sometimes just a phrase or a verbal talking prompt can inspire more conversation. You might develop the habit of whispering into a student's ear, "You might ask _____" or "You could say _____." Just remember that these phrases are scaffolds, and you want to make sure that students don't start waiting for you to tell them what to say before engaging in a conversation! If that pattern starts to happen, you'll want to dial back on the intervention and think about less-invasive ways to support students, such as written prompts they access themselves or a choice of a couple of different things to say.

PROVIDE WRITTEN PROMPTS OR QUESTION MENUS

If you pay attention to the way questions and responses tend to go in your classroom, then you can create menus of them that students can use as they develop their ability to have productive conversations. Folded paper stock works, as do two-sided picture frames or even individualized conversation cards. Possible starters could be:

Response Starters	Question Starters
I like how you _____.	Could it be _____?
I was confused when _____.	What were you thinking when _____?
I'm wondering if _____.	Have you considered _____?
This reminded me of _____.	

How Do I Support Student Thinking and Discussion Without Taking Over?

137

AGENCY

ASK FOR "THEIR OWN WORDS"

Any time you teach students something, you have the option of asking them to explain what you taught in their own words. "I understand this, and I can explain it," I say to students, "but ultimately, I'm not the one who needs to understand it. How would you explain it?" This question shifts agency to students at the end of your direct instruction. If it becomes a routine that students expect and understand, then it's likely that students will pay attention differently as you teach.

Notes

How Do I Engage Students in Self-Assessment?

John Hattie has conducted several meta-analyses that investigate and rank top indicators when it comes to learning. Self-assessment is consistently a top indicator (Waack, n.d.). Engagement means more than doing. More than ever, student engagement requires students being able to join the teacher in the cyclical process of self-assessment and goal-setting.

EXPECT SELF-ASSESSMENT DURING INSTRUCTION

While kidwatching is important when you are instructing, you can teach students to self-assess their understanding during instruction. If you have established a risk-taking environment where learning, and not mastery, is the norm, then you can ask students to communicate their understanding of a concept.

This is another opportunity for students to use their fists and fingers to self-assess. Students rate their understanding, holding up fingers to correlate with their understanding, as in the following chart:

Understanding Levels	
1	I'm confused and not ready to try this at all.
2	I understand a little, but I'm not ready to try it on my own.
3	I'll try, but I'm not sure it will be right.
4	I'm pretty sure I can do this on my own.
5	I can't wait to try it on my own.

This communication creates a feedback loop between you and the students, and based on their responses, you know whether to revisit the new learning with them.

ENCOURAGE SELF-ASSESSMENT OF INDEPENDENT WORK

Strong writing instruction includes significant time for independent writing, and that time should involve students working with intention. Assuming that they know what they are working on and why, then students also need to know how well they're doing, and the more resources they have, the more likely it is to happen. Furthermore, the more students understand and have examples of what work should look like, the more apt they are to create it. Therefore, you will want to develop a collection of mentor texts, exemplar texts, progressions, and checklists for students to use as guides.

- **Mentor texts** are usually published pieces of writing, although they don't have to be, that contain high-level craft moves students are trying to work on. You can annotate mentor texts so students not only name the targeted

AGENCY

skill but also notice the impact of it and pay attention to *how* the author did something. When students start noticing, then they may well start emulating, and that leads to increased student agency.

- **Exemplar texts** are student-written works that reflect and illustrate the skills you are hoping to see in their writing. Exemplar texts are especially effective because students often respond positively to seeing the work of peers. "If they can do it, then so can I" is a powerful mindset when it comes to learning. Additionally, exemplar texts can make new strategies more concrete and seem within reach. You can annotate exemplar texts in the same way you do mentor texts.

- **Progressions** help students analyze, compare, and contrast their own writing with a series of levels. As students move through grade levels, the expectations increase, but sometimes the expectations are so incremental that it's hard to understand the differences between the grade levels. Learning progressions help make those differences more visible so that students can see and understand what's expected. When students are able to identify the level of detail in their own writing with that of a sample in front of them, then they can make decisions about increasing and improving the levels right there on the spot for themselves.

- **Checklists** are useful tools for students as they are working toward effective self-assessment and agency. You can make your own checklists that reflect the language and skills you use within your own classroom, and that way, students (and you!) are more apt to understand and use them correctly. However, checklists require contemplation, intention, and honesty to be used effectively. It's tempting to check boxes without any reflection regarding the accuracy and validity of those checks. You will want to teach students to not only check boxes but also to be ready to explain where they used the specific skill. "Where is the evidence of that skill?" is a question you will want students to expect. They will begin to hold themselves responsible for a positive checkmark, and they will become more primed and ready for meaningful self-assessment.

Keep in Mind

Three questions provide important insights about student agency and the work they are doing:

- What or who helps you if you are stuck?

- What are you working on?

- How do you know if you're doing a good job?

How Can I Encourage Students to Set Goals and Decide on Next Steps?

Learning targets and student goal-setting lead to more student agency and consequently higher learning rates (Berger et al., 2014). Additionally, self-assessment correlates with stronger learning rates (Hattie & Clarke, 2019). It's important that students understand why they're learning something or setting a goal for attaining a new skill; this helps increase engagement and develop agency.

PROVIDE EXPLICIT INSTRUCTION ABOUT STUDENT GOAL-SETTING

Goal-setting will benefit students across multiple domains of their lives if they understand what the process entails. It's worth taking the time to teach the process.

Develop charts like the ones shown below to help students think about and discuss important questions: *What is a goal? What helps achieve a goal? What gets in the way of achieving a goal? How do we set ourselves up to be successful?* The answers to these questions vary for experienced goal-setters and brand-new ones.

Figures 5.5 and 5.6 Goal-setting charts provide visual reminders for students of their role in the learning process.

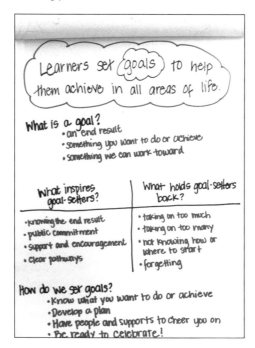

How Can I Encourage Students to Set Goals and Decide on Next Steps?

141

AGENCY

Announcing goals creates pressure that not everyone likes. Daily reminders might be a better system of accountability for some students. Some people thrive with goal partners, and other people may need more reinforcement along their goal-achieving pathway. Goal-setting patterns evolve as students feel more comfortable. Maybe they weren't ready to publicize their goals initially, but they become more comfortable as the year continues and the sense of community builds.

OFFER CHOICES AND RESOURCES FOR STUDENTS TO WORK ON THEIR GOALS

With an understanding of goals in place, you can set up systems for students to communicate their goals and seek out instruction that will help them. Some ways to establish that communication cycle include:

- Keyrings of choices that students choose from (see Figure 5.7)
- Charts where students can place name-sticks (see Figure 5.8)
- T-charts that students can use to note what they've seen and where they saw it (see Figure 5.9)
- Personal charts that students fill out and reference (see Figure 5.10)
- A checklist or multiple-choice question set that includes a list of skills students can select. (See Figure 5.11; a sample is linked in the companion website, resources.corwin.com/answerselementarywriting.)

Figure 5.7 Keyrings of choices that students choose from.

Figure 5.8 Charts where students can place name-sticks.

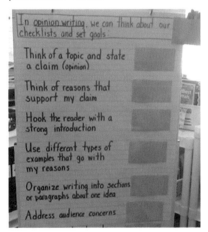

Figure 5.9 T-charts that students can use to note what they've seen and where they saw it.

What I noticed and Want To do	Who did it Where I Saw it
- Great Beginning	- EO's Writing
- Power of Three	- Yard sale
- Perfect Puntuation	- Jonah

Figure 5.10 Personal charts that students fill out and reference.

Figure 5.11 A checklist or multiple-choice question set that includes a list of skills students can select.

Please let me know what you've mastered as a writer and what you'd like to work on

Sign in to Google to save your progress. Learn more

Name

Your answer

Date

Date

mm/dd/yyyy

Skills I feel comfortable with:

☐ Coming up with ideas for writing

☐ Making a plan

☐ Knowing my beginning, middle, and end

☐ Using transition words

☐ Using paragraphs as I draft

☐ Explaining or elaborating my writing

☐ Using conventions

☐ Writing in complete sentences

☐ Spelling words correctly that I should

☐ Option 2

How Can I Encourage Students to Set Goals and Decide on Next Steps?

143

AGENCY

INVITE STUDENTS INTO THE PLANNING PROCESS FOR INDIVIDUAL AND SMALL GROUP INSTRUCTION

Chapter 3 is about the various forms of instruction, including various ways to plan and form small group and individualized instruction. While teachers should be reading, analyzing, and assessing student work to make instructional decisions, they can also invite students into the process. When students are setting goals, they are also helping teachers plan targeted instruction; when students have similar goals, you have a group!

Elementary students appreciate the term *seminars* because it implies a level of sophistication and high expectation, but the reality is that a seminar is small group instruction. Students can sign up for seminars that may include specific skills such as capitalizing or using transition words, as well as writing behaviors, such as ways to take charge of our own learning. Presenting sticky notes with the titles of available seminars work is a quick way to provide an effective system that involves students (see Figures 5.12 and 5.13). Digital sign-ups through a platform such as Jamboard also work.

Figures 5.12 and 5.13 Students can sign up for seminars on sticky notes.

 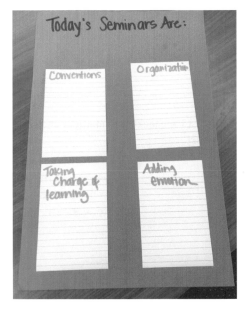

Source: Meehan & Sorum (2021).

The important element about inviting students to sign up for seminars is that students must self-assess to make decisions about what seminar to choose. Once they make that decision, then the seminar is reflective of their self-assessment, goal-setting, and intention to work on a specific element of writing.

End-of-Chapter Reflections

What might you try within the next week? The next month?

As you consider student agency, what elements feel strong and secure? What are some elements you consider opportunities for growth?

What are three goals that you are setting related to student agency?

How Can I Encourage Students to Set Goals and Decide on Next Steps?

145

AGENCY

REFERENCES

Ahmed, S. K. (2018). *Being the change lessons and strategies to teach social comprehension.* Heinemann.

Anderson, C. (2018). *A teacher's guide to writing conferences.* Heinemann.

Berger, R., Rugen, L., & Woodfin, L. (2014). *Leaders of their own learning: Transforming schools through student-engaged assessment.* Jossey-Bass.

Buckner, A. E. (2005). *Notebook know-how: Strategies for the writer's notebook.* Stenhouse.

Calkins, L., Hohne, K. B., & Robb, A. K. (2014). *Writing pathways: Performance assessments and learning progressions, grades K–8.* Heinemann.

CAST. (n.d.). *About Universal Design for Learning.* https://www.cast.org/impact/universal-design-for-learning-udl

Coppola, S. (2019). *Writing, redefined: Broadening our ideas of what it means to compose.* Stenhouse.

Corwin Visible Learning Meta. (2021, August). *Teacher clarity.* https://www.visiblelearningmetax.com/influences/view/teacher_clarity

Cozolino, L. J. (2013). *The social neuroscience of education: Optimizing attachment and learning in the classroom.* W. W. Norton & Company.

Culham, R. (2003). *6 + 1 traits of writing: The complete guide, grades 3 and up.* Scholastic.

Cunningham, K. E. (2019). *Start with joy: Designing literacy learning for student happiness.* Stenhouse.

Diller, D. (2021). *Simply small groups: Differentiating literacy learning in any setting.* Corwin.

Dorfman, L. R., Cappelli, R., & Hoyt, L. (2017). *Mentor texts: Teaching writing through children's literature, K–6.* Stenhouse.

Dweck, C. S. (2008). *Mindset: The new psychology of success.* Ballantine Books.

Edwards, K. (2021, May 19). The serious business of laughter in the classroom. *We Are Teachers.* https://www.weareteachers.com/laughter-in-the-classroom/

Fisher, D., & Frey, N. (2008). *Better learning through structured teaching: A framework for the gradual release of responsibility.* ASCD.

Fisher, D., & Frey, N. (2013). *Better learning through structured teaching: A framework for the gradual release of responsibility.* ASCD.

Fisher, D., & Frey, N. (2018, February 1). *Show & tell: A video column / A map for meaningful learning.* ASCD. https://www.ascd.org/el/articles/a-map-for-meaningful-learning

Fisher, D., Frey, N., Amador, O., & Assof, J. (2019). *The teacher clarity playbook: A hands-on guide to creating learning intentions.* Corwin.

Fisher, D., Frey, N., Hattie, J. (2016). *Visible learning for literacy, grades K–12: Implementing the practices that work best to accelerate student learning.* Corwin.

Fletcher, A. (2008). The architecture of ownership. *Educational Leadership* (66)3. https://www.ascd.org/el/articles/the-architecture-of-ownership

Fletcher, R. J. (2003). *A writer's notebook: Unlocking the writer within you.* HarperTrophy.

Gallo, A. (2012, November 12). How to master a new skill. *Harvard Business Review.* https://hbr.org/2012/11/how-to-master-a-new-skill

Goodman, Y. M. (1985). Kidwatching: Observing children in the classroom. In A. Jagger & M. T. Smith-Burke (Eds.), *Observing the language learner* (pp. 9–18). NCTE and IRA.

Graham, S. (2008). Writing assessment. *Encyclopedia of Special Education.* doi:10.1002/9780470373699.speced2243

Graham, S. (2019). Changing how writing is taught. *Review of Research in Education, 43*(1), 277–303. doi:10.3102/0091732x18821125

Graham, S., Gillespie, A., & McKeown, D. (2012). Writing: Importance, development, and instruction. *Reading and Writing, 26*(1), 1–15. doi:10.1007/s11145-012-9395-2

Graves. D. H. (n.d.a). *All children can write.* LD OnLine. http://www.ldonline.org/article/6204/

Graves, D. H. (n.d.b). *Answering your questions about teaching writing: A talk with Donald H. Graves.* Scholastic. https://www.scholastic.com/teachers/articles/teaching-content/answering-your-questions-about-teaching-writing-talk-donald-h-graves/

Graves, D. H. (2003). *Writing: Teachers and children at work*. Heinemann.

Hammond, Z. (2014). *Culturally responsive teaching and the brain: Promoting authentic engagement and rigor among culturally and linguistically diverse students*. Corwin.

Hammond, Z. (2021). *Integrating the science of learning and culturally responsive practice*. American Federation of Teachers. https://www.aft.org/ae/summer2021/hammond

Hargrave, M. (2020, February 26). The power of silent teachers: Helping writers increase productivity and build independence through interdependence with tools in the classroom. *Two Writing Teachers*. https://twowritingteachers.org/2020/02/26/hargrave/

Hattie, J. (2011). *Visible learning for teachers: Maximizing impact on learning*. Taylor & Francis.

Hattie, J., & Clarke, S. (2019, July). *On-your-feet guide to visible learning: Student-teacher feedback*. Corwin.

Hubbard, B. (2018, November 12). ICYMI: Notebooks as a writer's tool. *Two Writing Teachers*. https://twowritingteachers.org/2018/11/12/icymi-notebooks-as-a-writers-tool/

Koutrakos, P. A. (2022). *Mentor texts that multitask [grades K–8]: A less-is-more approach to integrated literacy instruction*. Corwin.

MacArthur, C. A. (2000). New tools for writing. *Topics in Language Disorders*, *20*(4), 85–100. https://doi.org/10.1097/00011363-200020040-00008

Marzano, R. J. (2009). *Classroom management that works: Research-based strategies for every teacher*. Pearson Education.

Marzano, R. J., Pickering, D. J., & Pollock, J. E. (2004). *Classroom instruction that works: Research-based strategies for increasing student achievement*. ASCD.

McGee, P. (2017). *Feedback that moves writers forward: How to escape correcting mode to transform student writing*. Corwin Literacy.

Medina, M. (2020a). *Evelyn Del Rey is moving away*. Candlewick Press.

Medina, M. (2020b). *Tía Isa wants a car*. Candlewick Press.

Medina, M. (2021). *Mango, abuela, and me*. Candlewick Press.

Meehan, M. (2019). *Every child can write, grades 2–5: Entry points, bridges, and pathways for striving writers*. Corwin.

Meehan, M., & Peterson, G. (2019, May 20). Bringing humor into writing workshops. *Two Writing Teachers*. https://twowritingteachers.org/2019/05/20/bringing-humor-into-writing-workshops/

Meehan, M., & Sorum, K. (2021). *The responsive writing teacher: Aligning instruction to the writers in your classroom*. Corwin.

Moore, B. (2021, March 18). Making space in writing workshop for kids to be funny. *Two Writing Teachers*. https://twowritingteachers.org/2021/03/18/making-space-for-kids-to-be-funny/

National Equity Project. (n.d.). *Educational equity: A definition*. https://www.nationalequityproject.org/education-equity-definition

Parker, F., Novak, J., & Bartell, T. (2017, September 25). To engage students, give them meaningful choices in the classroom. *Phi Delta Kappan*, *99*(2), 37–41. doi:10.1177/0031721717734188

Popham, W. J. (2011). *Classroom evidence of successful teaching, mastering assessment*. Allyn & Bacon.

Serravallo, J. (2010). *Teaching reading in small groups: Differentiated instruction for building strategic, independent readers*. Heinemann.

Serravallo, J. (2017). *The writing strategies book: Your everything guide to developing skilled writers*. Heinemann.

Serravallo, J. (2021). *Teaching writing in small groups*. Heinemann.

Shubitz, S. (2016). *Craft moves: Lesson sets for teaching writing with mentor texts*. Stenhouse.

Shubitz, S., & Dorfman, L. R. (2019). *Welcome to writing workshop: Engaging today's students with a model that works*. Stenhouse.

Sokolowski, K. N. (2021, August 3). Creating community: Our favorite things. *Two Writing Teachers*. https://twowritingteachers.org/2021/08/03/ways-to-create-community-our-favorite-things/

Spilling, E. F., Rønneberg, V., Rogne, W. M., Roeser, J., & Torrance, M. (2021). Handwriting versus keyboarding: Does writing modality affect quality of narratives written by beginning writers? *Reading and Writing*. https://doi.org/10.1007/s11145-021–10169-y

Stockman, A. (2021, May 11). Supporting multimodal composition in the writing workshop: Simple ways to begin. *Two Writing Teachers*. https://twowritingteachers.org/2021/05/26/stockman-2/

Trumbull, E., & Lash, A. (2013). *Understanding formative assessment insights from learning theory and measurement theory*. WestEd. https://www.wested.org/resources/understanding-formative-assessment-insights-from-learning-theory-and-measurement-theory/

Vygotsky, L. S. (1978). *Mind in society: The development of higher psychological processes*. Harvard University Press.

Waack, S. (n.d.). *Glossary of Hattie's influences on student achievement*. Visible Learning. https://visible-learning.org/glossary/

Wagner, T. (2012). *Creating innovators: The making of young people who will change the world*. Scribner.

Wittgenstein, L. (2010). *Tractatus logico-philosophicus* (C. K. Ogden, Trans.). Kegan Paul. (Original work published 1921) https://www.gutenberg.org/files/5740/5740-pdf.pdf

Wright, J. T., & Hoonan, B. (2018). *What are you grouping for? How to guide small groups based on readers—not the book*. Corwin.

Zeiser, K., Scholz, C., & Cirks, V. (2018, October). *Maximizing student agency: Implementing and measuring student-centered learning practices*. American Institutes for Research. https://files.eric.ed.gov/fulltext/ED592084.pdf

INDEX

Answers to Your Biggest Questions About Teaching Elementary Writing

Because...

ALL TEACHERS ARE LEADERS

DOMINIQUE SMITH, DOUGLAS FISHER, NANCY FREY
Take an active approach toward disrupting the negative effects of labels and assumptions that interfere with student learning.

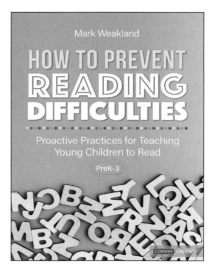

MARK WEAKLAND
Build on decades of evidence and years of experience to understand how the brain learns to read and how to apply that understanding to Tier 1 instruction.

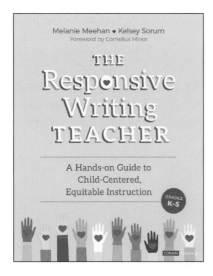

MELANIE MEEHAN, KELSEY SORUM
Learn how to adapt curriculum to meet the needs of the whole child. Each chapter offers intentional steps for responsive instruction across four domains: academic, linguistic, cultural, and social-emotional.

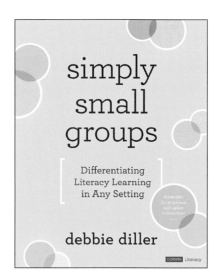

DEBBIE DILLER
Discover concrete guidance for tailoring the small-group experience to literacy instruction in order to give every reader a pathway to success.

To order your copies, visit corwin.com/literacy

At Corwin Literacy we have put together a collection of just-in-time, classroom-tested, practical resources from trusted experts that allow you to quickly find the information you need when you need it.

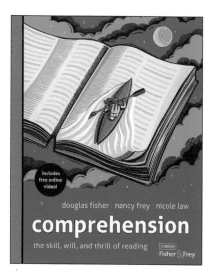

DOUGLAS FISHER, NANCY FREY, NICOLE LAW

Using a structured, three-pronged approach—skill, will, and thrill—students experience reading as a purposeful act with this new comprehensive model of reading instruction.

PAM KOUTRAKOS

Packed with ready-to-go lessons and tools, this user-friendly resource provides ways to weave together different aspects of literacy using one mentor text.

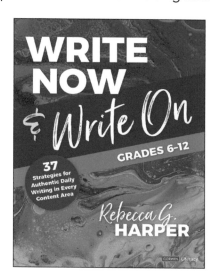

REBECCA G. HARPER

Customizable strategies turn students' informal writing into a springboard for daily writing practice in every content area—with a focus on academic vocabulary, summarizing, and using textual evidence.

MELANIE MEEHAN, CHRISTINA NOSEK, MATTHEW JOHNSON, DAVE STUART JR., MATTHEW R. KAY

This series offers actionable answers to your most pressing questions about teaching reading, writing, and ELA.

A SAGE Publishing Company

CORWIN HAS ONE MISSION: to enhance education through intentional professional learning.

We build long-term relationships with our authors, educators, clients, and associations who partner with us to develop and continuously improve the best evidence-based practices that establish and support lifelong learning.